OUTSTANDING
BLACK SERMONS

Volume 3

OUTSTANDING BLACK SERMONS

Volume 3

Milton E. Owens, Jr., editor

Judson Press ® Valley Forge

OUTSTANDING BLACK SERMONS, VOLUME 3
Copyright © 1982
Judson Press, Valley Forge, PA 19482-0851
Third Printing, 1988

Unless otherwise indicated, Bible quotations in this volume are from *The Holy Bible*, King James Version.

Other quotations of the Bible are from the Revised Standard Version of the Bible copyrighted 1946, 1952 © 1971, 1973 by the Division of Christian Education of the National Council of the Churches of Christ in the U.S.A., and used by permission.

Library of Congress Cataloging in Publication Data (Revised)
Main entry under title:

Outstanding Black sermons.

  Vol. 2 edited by W. B. Hoard; vol. 3 edited by Milton E. Owens, Jr.
  Includes bibliographical references.
  1. Sermons, American—Afro-American.
I. Smith, J. Alfred (James Alfred) II. Hoard, Walter B. III. Owens, Milton E.
BV4241.5.09   252'.08996073   76-2084
ISBN 0-8170-0664-8 (v. 1)   ISBN 0-8170-0973-6 (v.3)

The name JUDSON PRESS is registered as a trademark in the U.S. Patent Office.
Printed in the U.S.A. ⊕

Contents

84/92

Introduction

The church continues to be the principal institution of black America. It is a place of comfort, encouragement, joy, and hope for a people still struggling to be free from the subtle and overt forms of dehumanization that persistently haunt black folk. In the 1860s and the 1960s there was a glimmer of hope that the political and economic institutions would deliver black people from the ranks of the disinherited into the mainstream of social and economic opportunity. In time the bright lights of full participation in the marketplace began to yield to the darkness of the night.

As we chart our course for surviving the dark days of the 1980s, we see even more clearly that the church is the principal institution of black America just as it was in the 1880s. Its choirs continue to sing the songs of Zion; its boards continue to lead; and its auxiliary groups continue to minister to "the least of these." What does the black church have that other social and political institutions find wanting? What is the dominant characteristic of the black church that causes folk to cling to it in good times and bad? I believe it is preaching.

Black preaching is a verbal, emotional experience that addresses the fears, hopes, guilt, joy, pain, and faith of the individual and the community. Preaching is a very awesome task. The preacher is called to pREACH, to prEACH, and preACH(E). The sermons in this volume reflect a variety of styles of pREACHING to the people of God. ○

Milton E. Owens, Jr.

When a Hunch Pays Off

Charles E. Booth

2 Kings 5:1-16

The Introduction

There are some things that time never changes. In every generation people have been enamored with those who possess rank, power, prestige, and position. The powerful of this generation are the athletes, movie stars, singers, and other performers of the arts. People will stand in line just to get a glimpse of these celebrities whether it is in the biting chill of the winter or the humid heat of the summer. However, it is a fact that military heroes and statesmen have a particular and secure place in the affections of people the world

Dr. Charles E. Booth is pastor of the Mount Olivet Baptist Church, Columbus, Ohio. His many community involvements include the Board of Trustees, Lincoln Cultural Arts Center; the Board of Black Campus Ministry, Ohio State University; the General Board of the Ohio Council of Churches. He has been the guest preacher for the National Baptist Churches of South Africa and the Central Panama Baptist Association. In 1980 he was listed in *Outstanding Young Men in America*. Dr. Booth is a graduate of Howard University, Washington, D.C.; Eastern Baptist Theological Seminary, Philadelphia, Pennsylvania; and he received the honorary Doctor of Divinity degree from Lynchburg College, Lynchburg, Virginia.

over—Eisenhower, Patton, MacArthur, Churchill, Roosevelt, Truman, Dulles, Kissinger, Begin, and Sadat, just to name a few. These are personalities who live on in our remembrance because they have made or are continuing to make significant contributions not only to the nations they represent but also to the world order.

Naaman, captain of the Syrian host, was such a renowned figure. He was a great man admired by the masses. He was a military commander who had marched triumphantly many times into Syrian cities and had experienced victory after victory. Naaman was a champion among his people, an honorable human specimen of integrity. However, his legacy does not stop with all of these positive pronouncements. The concluding word on Naaman declares, ". . .but he was a leper." He was captain of the Syrian host, but he was a leper. He was a great man, but he was a leper. He was honorable, but he was a leper. He was a mighty man of valor, but he was a leper.

"But." That awful conjunction always suggests that however grand and glorious we may be, there is something wrong with us. There are no perfect specimens in the human race. We each have our faults and failures. There is something terrifyingly and tragically wrong with each of us. Like Naaman, everybody lives with a limp. Richard Nixon was well versed in world diplomacy, but there was Watergate. Jimmy Carter was a born-again president, but his domestic policies left a lot to be desired. Henry Kissinger was a great secretary of state, but there were those secret raids in Cambodia. Franklin Delano Roosevelt was a great president, but he had polio. Lyndon Baines Johnson gave us the "Great Society," but there was Vietnam. Joe Louis was the heavyweight champion of the world, but he died broken in body and finances. Paul was a great apostle, but he had a thorn in his flesh. Peter was a great fisherman, but he denied Jesus three times. Neither you nor I can escape it. There is a "but" in our lives also.

I

Naaman had leprosy, the most dreaded disease of the biblical era. His body frame, once the splendor of his masculinity, was now covered with spots and scabs and a white swelling of the skin. His hair was beginning to change in color from dark to a white or tainted shade of yellow. People were now running away from him instead of to him.

He was no longer cheered as he walked among his people. Rather, people shuddered when they gazed upon his leprous condition.

Whatever the "but" in life, the believer in God never relinquishes the hope or the expectation that God can reverse any negative situation. If he does not remove the burden, he will strengthen the shoulder on which the burden is borne. Sometimes God will work through someone else who has a higher quality of faith. Sometimes the answer to our problems resides in others whose faith far outdistances our own. Many of us are where we are today not because of our goodness or prayers but because of the diligent prayers of some parent or guardian who had laid us before the consciousness of God.

So it was with Naaman. The answer to his leprosy resided in the declaration of some nameless little maid who happened to be talking with Naaman's wife. "There is a prophet in Samaria who can cure him of his leprosy." This was her declaration. He is not educated, but he is consecrated. He is not sophisticated, but he is dedicated. He is not an erudite scholar. He is not a physician or a pharmaceutical expert. He is not a military commander. His name is not a household word, but he is a prophet of the most high God, a man with unusual spiritual and healing power. His name is Elisha, and he is the prophetic successor to the great Elijah whom the Lord took home in a chariot of fire down by the Jordan. It is upon Elisha that Elijah's mantle has fallen, and he received a double portion of Elijah's power. It was Elijah who pronounced the three and a half year famine in Israel. It was Elijah whom the Lord fed by the brook Cherith. It was Elijah who defeated the four hundred and fifty prophets of Baal and slayed them by the brook Keshon. It was Elijah who stopped the messengers of Ahaziah and pronounced the end of the young king's life. "There is a prophet, a man of God, who can assist your husband in the ridding of his malady."

How tragic it is that we live in a disbelieving generation. We have minimized the church as well as the influence and power of the preacher. If the man of God is genuine, authentic, called of God, and dug up by the ploughshares of the gospel, he can still perform miraculous feats in the name of the Lord of Hosts. Many want to cast the old preacher aside because the years have taken away his youth, energy, vitality, and luster. May we never forget how the Lord has used the preacher in our lives and how God can still do so. However young or old we might be, God can work through a man or a woman if that individual is willing to be a conduit, channel, vessel, or instrument through which the unction might flow.

How often does a military commander take the advice of a nameless handmaiden? Not often, but Naaman did in this case. He had no choice. All else in Syria had failed. He was now at rock bottom. This was only a hunch, a possibility. Very often life demands that we take a chance, a leap of faith. What did Naaman have to lose? A prominent psychologist has suggested that a man can survive without bread and water for unusual periods of time, but if he has no hope, he will perish immediately. Paul is correct when he says, "Faith is the substance of things hoped for, the evidence of things not seen" (Hebrews 11:1).

II

Whenever one takes a chance in life, one must be careful to listen intently and carefully to the guiding instructions. The little maid said, "There is a prophet in Samaria who can cure Naaman of his leprosy." Naaman went to the king instead of the prophet, thinking, undoubtedly, that the two were synonymous. Prophet and king are not the same! The king is a statesman, and the prophet is the man of God. The king is a political instrument, and the prophet has his secret closet. The king commands marching armies, and the prophet can call on legions of angels. The king has a scepter of power in his hands, and the prophet has a trumpet down in his soul, "Father, I Stretch My Hands to Thee." It is no wonder that the king of Israel rent his clothes and informed Naaman that he had consulted the wrong man. "It is not the king that you need; it's the man of God."

What a lesson for the nation today! Ronald Reagan is not God! The Congress is not God! Judges and judicial bodies are not God! We need the church today more than ever before! If Reagan is insensitive to minority needs, if the Congress is insensitive to minority needs, if judiciaries are going to knock out busing decrees and affirmative action programs, then we have no choice but to seek our heavenly Father. He still sits high and looks low. He still can destroy and defend. He can still make a way out of no way. He can still provide manna in the wilderness. He can still open the Red Sea. He can still deliver us from the lion's den and the fiery furnace. He can still feed us when we get hungry, give water to us when we are thirsty, and clothe us when we are naked. We need the *church!*

III

Naaman had to leave the plush court of the king and find the humble abode of the prophet. The cure was simple, "Go and wash in Jordan seven times, and thy flesh shall come again to thee, and thou shalt be clean." Naaman abhorred this suggestion because the Jordan was a muddy old river. There were cleaner rivers.

Sometimes God must humble us before he can use us. Does not history teach us the lesson that quite often the mighty must be brought low so that the glory of the Lord shall be revealed?

> Every valley shall be exalted, and every mountain and hill shall be made low: and the crooked shall be made straight, and the rough places plain: And the glory of the Lord shall be revealed, and all flesh shall see it together: for the mouth of the Lord hath spoken it (Isaiah 40:4-5).

Naaman had to learn that it is only when you are knocked down that you can be raised up. It is only when you are humbled that you can be exalted. It is only when you go down that you can come up. It is only when you cry that you can appreciate laughter. It is only when you are broken that you can be made whole. It is only when you are dirty that you can be made clean. It is only when you are crucified that you can be resurrected.

"Go and wash seven times in the Jordan." Seven is the number of divine fullness, perfection, and completion. There are seven days in the week. The Bible says there were seven men who lived to be more than nine hundred years old. In the Revelation of Saint John the Divine, there are seven churches, seven angels, seven dooms, seven seals, and seven trumpets. Jesus uttered seven last words from the cross of Calvary. Naaman had to dip seven times.

> *One for the patriarchs!*
> *One for the prophets!*
> *One for the judges!*
> *One for the apostles!*
> *One for the Father!*
> *One for the Son!*
> *One for the Holy Ghost!*

And Naaman was made whole! The same is true for anyone who will do precisely what the Lord instructs! ○

Magnificent Obsession

Albert F. Campbell

Nehemiah 6:1-9

Some psychologists and psychiatrists and other students of human behavior would doubtless agree that an obsession is a type of insanity.

In fact, as I have searched *Roget's Thesaurus*, I find that obsession is a synonym for lunacy, derangement, delirium, dementia, idiocy. All of these are said to mean the same thing as obsession.

But I was not satisfied with the synonyms for the term "obsession" as *Roget's Thesaurus* set them forth.

Looking further, I peered into *The Britannica World Language Dictionary* for a broader definition of the term "obsession." There I discovered that an obsession is, "A compulsive *idea* or *emotion*, associated with the subconscious, and exerting a more-or-less persistent influence upon conduct and behavior."

Rev. Albert F. Campbell is the pastor of the Mount Carmel Baptist Church, Philadelphia, Pennsylvania, and is an adjunct professor at Eastern Baptist College, St. Davids, Pennsylvania. He is an alumnus of Bishop College, Dallas, Texas, and Union Theological Seminary, New York, New York. He has served on the Board of Directors, Philadelphia Baptist Association, American Baptist Churches in the U.S.A.; the Executive Committee, Foreign Mission Board, National Baptist Convention, U.S.A., Inc.; and is a member of the Board of Directors for the United Fund of Greater Philadelphia.

It is, therefore, precisely in this latter sense, rather than the former, that I use the term "obsession"! And my preference for the latter definition is not so much because it absolutely denies that obsession can mean insanity but simply because it does not equate all obsession with insanity.

If obsession were, indeed, a type of insanity and the tendency were characteristic of all of us, then we ought to strive to make our obsession a magnificent one.

Nehemiah, the prophet of the Lord, was magnificently obsessed, preeminently preoccupied. A glorious and wonderful idea compulsively controlled him! A majestic dream persuasively possessed him! A valiant and vibrant vision exerted conspicuous and persistent influence upon his conduct and behavior.

The compelling idea and compulsive influence expressed themselves verbally in the message that Nehemiah sent back to his enemies, his foes, "I am doing a great work and I cannot come down. Why should the work stop while I leave it and come down to you? And they sent to me four times in this way and I answered them in the same manner: I am doing a great work, and I cannot come down.

"Why should the work stop while I leave it and come down to you?" (Nehemiah 6:3-4, RSV).

I

Nehemiah was being used by an idea whose time had come!

We sometimes hear it said of some very brilliant people in many fields that they failed to achieve their true level of greatness because they were "ahead of their time." Which is to say, either their ideas and visions and dreams far exceeded their grasp, or else history, the world, mankind was not ready for the proper acceptance of their dreams and visions and ideas.

There may well be some modicum of truth in such a claim, and I am not prepared to argue the question one way or another! But here in our text is the towering testimony of a man who did not simply use an idea but rather let himself be used by an idea whose time had come!

The circumstances of history and of his own life situation had combined to thrust Nehemiah into a role of responsible leadership. He was destined by God and designated by the compassionate king, Artaxerxes, to return to Jerusalem from Babylonian exile, to rebuild the Jerusalem walls and the Jerusalem temple!

Now, it occurred to Nehemiah to measure meekly his limited tools and talents over against the enormity of such a task. It may even have occurred to him to ponder deeply the proposition of whether he or perhaps another was better suited to match the magnitude of such a moment.

It had happened before with Moses at the burning bush. There, at that pivotal place and point in time, Moses argued with the Lord that he was inarticulate and ill-equipped while others were far better equipped to go and face and tell Pharaoh to "Let God's people go!"

In Nehemiah's case there may well have been some others who were less well suited but wanted to lead or who were better suited to lead in the rebuilding process but failed to come forward.

At any rate, the moment of truth rested with Nehemiah. It was he and not another who had ". . .come to the kingdom for such a time as this." It was God's idea, history's dream, and Nehemiah's compulsion that brought him to the task of rebuilding the Jerusalem walls. It was providentially the time, and Nehemiah was the man. Whatever his ambitions or his reservations, Nehemiah let the idea use him for God's and history's purpose.

II

It should be borne in mind also that no matter how magnificent an obsession and no matter how obediently people may let themselves be used by an idea whose time has come, such an obsession gets them in trouble even as it did Nehemiah!

So long as Nehemiah's dream remained in his own mind or just on paper or in the mere talking and planning stage, as it were, the response was generally mixed.

Some, perhaps, said, "He's a fine fellow, and his notion is a noble one."

Others, perhaps, said, "It is a laudible idea, a fine dream, but it is also an impossible dream."

Others, still, may just have been waiting to see what Nehemiah was going to do, to see if he would show some progress! If he evidenced some measure of success, then they would join him!

There are all too many people who are thrown into a situation of promise and possibility but who delay or prevent the promise and possibility from being readily realized or make it unrealized altogether simply because they are waiting, waiting to see what happens, waiting to see which way the wind will blow! They don't want to be identified with failure, but they do want to be a part of the success story if there is one. Their religion, their morality, their politics, their human and community concern are all of the bandwagon variety. And precisely because they don't want to be associated with failure and yet want to be on the winning team, they must wait! They have to wait to see what happens! They have to wait to see what happens because they have to keep their options open! If there is a modicum of failure, they want to be able to say, "I told you so!" If there is a measure of success, they also want to be able to say, "Look what we have done!"

In Nehemiah's case, no sooner had the rebuilding program begun to proceed on schedule and there was some noticeable degree of success, when a lot of folks started laying traps and digging ditches for him instead of getting on board. That is to say, as Nehemiah began and continued to build, opposition began and continued to build also! What was thought to be an idea well worth embracing for all became a sore spot for Nehemiah's enemies, his foes!

As much as everybody likes the "sweet smell of success," success also has the uncanny capacity to separate friends from foes! Of course, failure can do this, too, but success has a kind of double-barreled effect! Success not only has a way of separating friends from foes, but it also has a way of making the opposition more forceful and formidable, more determined and more cunning in its determination to block growth and impede progress.

That is why all true servants of God have to understand that God's kingdom economy is based on the gold standard, gold tried in fire. And the furnace fire standards of measuring success in the kingdom are quite different from those standards by which the world measures success. The Lord never commanded his disciples to "be successful," but he did admonish his followers to "be faithful unto death" because it is faithfulness and not successfulness that guarantees the crown of life.

So, if you have a dream but you are not willing to run the risk of making some enemies by putting foundations under it, then your dream is likely to end up on the garbage heap of wasted dreams.

If you have a vision of God, of Christ, and of the kingdom of God but you are too timid to run the risk of becoming an object of crucifixion, then your vision is too small! At best, it is not a magnificent one!

Nehemiah's enemies hurled everything they could at him. They pleaded with him; they criticized him; they cajoled him! They stretched the truth; they fabricated lies; they plotted to trap him away from home; they sent threatening letters; they accused him on false charges, trying to lure him down!

In each and every instance, his response was consistently the same, "I am doing a great work and I cannot come down. Why should the work stop while I leave it and come down to you?"

Nehemiah was not magnificent. He was motivated by a magnificent idea. He was not fearless, he was faithful; and his fullness of faith enabled him to control his fears! He had his troubles, troubles aplenty, but he refused to let his troubles trouble him, i.e. get him down! He was claimed by a firm and unswerving sense of social and moral and religious responsibility. He was magnificently obsessed!

III

Magnificent obsessions are lasting. They never die! A dream deferred, a dream delayed, is not a dream dead!

You can kill the dreamer but not the dream. You can destroy the visionary, but the vision survives. John had a dream! Martin had a dream! Bobby had a dream! And they killed them! But surely their dreams are not dead!

Nehemiah was magnificently obsessed! His enemies disturbed and distressed him, deferred and delayed his dream's fulfillment. But, in God's own time, his dream was brought to fruition. And somebody asked, "Who . . . saw this house in its first glory? And how do you see it now? . . . The latter splendor of this house shall be greater than the former!" (Haggai 2:3-9, RSV).

Magnificent obsessions cannot die because they are contagious. Even a single individual who is gripped by a compelling and divinely ordained idea manages somehow to communicate that same compelling idea to those who come in contact with him!

Nehemiah's testimony was, "So we built the wall; and all the wall was joined together to half its height. For the people had a mind to work." Nehemiah's magnificent obsession was contagious. The people caught the same spirit because Nehemiah communicated it by his high resolve!

Because magnificent obsessions are both lasting and contagious, Nehemiah is not alone in history. He had and does have his contemporaries who have been and are equally claimed by a compelling and glorious idea!

Abraham was Nehemiah's spiritual contemporary. He left the comforts of his geographical and cultural roots and his familiar surroundings, not knowing where he was to go. He was searching for a city which had foundations, whose builder and maker was God. When, for all practical purposes, he should not have gone, he went anyway, believing that God would show him the time and the place for the fulfillment of his dream.

Moses, like Nehemiah, was magnificently obsessed also. We are told that "By faith Moses, when he was grown up, refused to be called the son of Pharoah's daughter, choosing rather to share ill-treatment with the people of God than to enjoy the fleeting pleasures of sin" (Hebrews 11:24-25, RSV).

The Master himself, the Master of all men, was Nehemiah's contemporary. He, too, was claimed and used by an idea come of age. The New Testament calls it the kingdom, the kingdom of God, the kingdom of heaven! Christ's consuming passion was the kingdom! Christ's consumate desire was to do the will of his Father to whom the kingdom ultimately belonged. He said, "I must be about my Father's business!" (Luke 2:49). "I must work the works of him that sent me, while it is day: the night cometh when no man can work" (John 9:4). "I must go to Jerusalem, and suffer, and be killed and be raised again the third day!" (See Matthew 16:21 and Luke 9:22).

Nehemiah was in very excellent company then when in the face of formidable temptation, formidable opposition, formidable odds, in the face of formidable suggestions of compromise he responded, "I am doing a great work and I cannot come down! Why should the work stop while I leave it and come down to you?"

I thank God that many, both before and since his time, have caught the same spirit as Nehemiah, the spirit of the magnificently obsessed.

And should you happen to be among those who have not caught it and have not been claimed by it, I suggest you do catch the spirit and be claimed by it now! ○

Do You Love Me?

Yvonne V. Delk

John 21:1-19

The Reality of the Resurrection

Two thousand years ago Jesus' disciples stood on a shore, trying to ascertain the meaning of the resurrection and the authority that it held for their lives. Jesus had appeared to them since his death and resurrection, but his appearance was like a vision. The reality of his resurrection was not firmly fixed in their minds, hearts, and souls. Therefore, they were experiencing anxiety about their future, their identity, and their ministry and mission in life.

In this time of anxiety and uncertainty the disciples returned to the trade that they knew and had practiced before meeting Jesus. They

Dr. Yvonne V. Delk is the Affirmative Action officer, the United Church of Christ. She has been a member of the faculty at Andover Newton Theological School, Harvard Divinity School, and the Black Theological Coalition of the Boston Theological Institute. Dr. Delk is a graduate of Norfolk State College, Norfolk, Virginia; Andover Newton Theological Seminary, Newton Centre, Massachusetts; and New York Theological Seminary, New York, New York, where she received the Doctor of Ministry degree. She is a member of the Board of Trustees for Andover Newton Theological School, the Metropolitan New York Project Equality, and New York Theological Seminary. In 1974 Dr. Delk was ordained as a minister in the United Church of Christ and is the recipient of the denomination's Antoinette Brown award.

returned to their old ways. They went back to fishing. However, fishing without a perspective, without an identity, without a future hope can yield very little. The journey back to their old way of life was not very productive until Jesus, the source of their authority, entered the picture.

Jesus called to them, helped them to get a fix on their situation so that they could fill their nets, and waited for them to join him on the shore. Once they recognized Jesus, they knew that the risen Lord was not a figment of their imagination nor the appearance of a spirit or a ghost. They knew without a doubt that it was Jesus, who had conquered death and had returned. Once they were on the shore, they could see him clearly, touch the nailprints in his hands and feet, and see the imprint of the crown of thorns in his brow. There was no doubt that this was Jesus, the risen Lord, because he bore the marks of pain and suffering on a cross. He also reflected the joy that emerges when one is able to transcend death.

Jesus kindled a fire for them, prepared a meal, and communed with them. After a time of remembering the past three years with the disciples, he turned to Simon and posed a question, "Simon, son of Jonas, do you love me more than these?"

Jesus asked this question three times. One commentary suggests that Jesus asked the question three times because Simon had denied him three times. In his gracious forgiveness Jesus gave Simon the chance to wipe out the memory of a threefold denial by giving him the chance to make a threefold declaration of love. The declaration of love brought with it a task, and it brought a cross. It also brought three opportunities for Simon to give his life in service.

Two thousand years have passed since Jesus appeared to his disciples, and we are called to give witness to the reality of that resurrection in our time and to make it incarnate in our lives.

We are called at a time in which the religious impulse is strong in our nation. Some see this as the Fourth Great Awakening since the current popularity of Neo-Evangelicalism has resulted in the claim of fifty million born-again Christians.

We are called at a time in which there is a conscious move on the part of many in our nation to the right, to conservatism, to a privatized fundamental religion that leaves behind any memory of the cost of discipleship.

We are called at a time when our future is uncertain. People are seeking meaning and belonging as never before, for it is a time in which identities are insecure and power bases are shifting.

We are called in an age of scarcity. We are called in an age of nuclear power. We are called in an age of increased violence.

We are called at a time in which people are turning inward. They are losing their ground in community. The sense of collective responsibility for the fate of each separate other is waning.

What takes the place of collective responsibility is a moral vacuum in which others are trapped forever in a private destiny, doomed to whatever befalls them. In that void the traditional measure of justice or good vanishes completely. The self replaces community, relatives, neighbors, or God. The end result of this retreat from the complexities of this world is the denial, in the name of higher truth, of the claims of others upon self. What is lost is human community.

The questions for us who respond to God's care are:

- How do we tell the story in a time of change, anxiety, and insecurity?
- How do we communicate the relevance of Jesus' love, death, and resurrection to this society?
- Can we proclaim the Good News for persons and systems in a manner that transforms rather than defends the status quo?

We, like the disciples who stood by the Sea of Tiberias, also find ourselves in the postresurrection period. What does it mean for us to confess a risen Lord? Who are we in light of the resurrection? Does the resurrection give us the courage to lay down some old names in order to give birth to the new? Can we lay down the names of racist, sexist, classist, imperialist, and elitist in order to give birth to a community that is truly inclusive and pluralistic?

If the reality of the resurrection is firmly fixed in our hearts, minds, and souls, what is it that we are prepared to leave behind in order to follow Christ? Simon had to leave behind the boats, the nets, the treasured art of fishing in order to become a shepherd who would feed the lambs and the sheep. What is the excess baggage that we must abandon? Does our baggage include the treasured self-images from which we have gotten a lot of mileage? When we take a serious look at ourselves, we are cast into roles partly chosen and partly imposed. The voice comes to us just as it came to Simon and to the disciples, "Leave your precious things behind and follow me." Leave the security that enslaves you and head for the freedom in the wilderness.

It's hard to move out. More often, we turn away, clutching our great possessions. We struggle with the call to leave and the yearning to stay. Each new day to live, each new place to enter, each new relationship to embrace requires departures from treasured old things and precious old patterns. Do we love and trust God enough to abandon the old and engage the new possibilities. If our answer is yes, then there will be tasks and responsibilities, and for some there will be a cross. Equally important, there will be the opportunity to move out on a promise and to join God in creating a vision of justice, wholeness, and peace.

In addition to being a people of the resurrection, we are a people who must face the meaning of the question that Jesus raised with Simon for our lives and our ministry.

Simon, Son of Jonas, Do You Love Me More Than These?

Jesus addressed Simon by name within the context of his bloodline, his culture, his experience. The call for ministry can, therefore, be seen as a personal call that addresses us as persons within the context of our names, our histories, our experiences, our pains, our joys, our stories. The call affirms us as persons of worth and meaning. The call by name assures us that we do not have to be invisible but informs us that we are affirmed and validated by God. Our power and authority, therefore, come from God who has called us by name into existence. Once we know that we have been called by name, no one can ever reduce us to namelessness again.

If God calls us by name, we do not have to cast ourselves into the image of anyone else. We do not have to live out the identity of another. We don't have to preach or pray or sing or model our ministry as anybody else. We only have to be faithful to the Word that has been incarnated in us.

Jesus not only addressed Simon by name, but he also raised a question, "Do you love me?" A call to ministry involves the ability to feel deeply. It involves passion. Jesus did not want from Simon a head answer only. He wanted an answer that would flow out of a deep sense of caring, feeling, loving, pain, and joy. Jesus understood that people who feel deeply, who possess passion, will risk living and dying. People without passion do not live or die very well. They feel neither pain nor joy deeply. They are people who do not fully comprehend the meaning of the resurrection, for when people experience pain and joy, they understand the resurrection.

The question, "Do you love me?" can also be interpreted as,

"Simon, do you love me enough to make a commitment?" *The call to ministry is rooted in a commitment.* We live in the midst of a culture and society in which people have no past and no future. They live for what they can get, keep, have, use, and throw away. The American way of life is a desperate fling that yields no enduring joy because it's all throwaway. Handy throwawayness is what life is all about. Handy throwawayness is what corporations do with people; it is what clever people do with ideas; and it is what mobile people do with possessions. Use it up and get another one. Products are always being invented. When we have nothing else to draw on, we must get more things. Production and consumption become the order of the day.

The call to ministry is an invitation to choose an alternative history in which vows are given and promises are made. I believe that Christian nurture has to do with inviting people to become persons who can speak words, who can hear words, who can give gifts and who can receive gifts, who can make vows and trust vows, who can make promises and keep them. People who can make vows and commitments are people who move with a sense of interconnection, long-rangeness, and hope in life.

Finally, "Simon, son of Jonas, do you love me? Then feed my sheep." *A call to ministry is ultimately a call to service.* It is not admission to a particular sect or order. We cannot set apart, but we are set in the midst of community. We are not called to be alone but to be beside. The call to service offers an alternative notion of authority.

Jesus refused the authority of the society that promised more bread, more power, more prestige and status. He transcended the rules of authority. He lived in the world by a different set of definitions. He lived so that the system could not contain or domesticate him. He had the power to serve but not to master. He had the power to die but not to kill, the power to bring order but not to dominate.

We are not called to be successful, but we are called to be faithful. We are not authored by the law, by seminaries, by the pages of our resumes. We are authored by the voice of God who calls us by name into service.

Simon, son of Jonas, do you really love me? The question is a personal question addressed to each of us.

It calls us by name;
It calls us to be in touch with our passion;
It calls us to make a commitment;

It calls us to a life of service alongside and on behalf of those who are in need—in pain, in agony—in the worldwide community;

It calls us to affirm for our day the reality of the resurrection, to be a present-day witness of life that can overcome death.

For those of us who can give ourselves to the task, the world will be amazed at our deeds, for we have the promise that eyes have not seen, ears have not heard just what the Lord has in store for persons who can really love God. ○

The Battle of Bethlehem

James A. Forbes, Jr.

Brothers and sisters, I want to speak to you today about the hero of the Battle of Bethlehem. Don't be embarrassed if you have not noticed this particular battle in your readings about the great battles in world history, for it does not appear in most of the lists. Indeed, I must acknowledge that I only became aware of this battle very recently when reading, more closely than I usually do, the words of Phillips Brooks' "O Little Town of Bethlehem."

Dr. James A. Forbes, Jr., is an associate professor of worship and homiletics, Union Theological Seminary, New York, New York, and is chairman of the education department, United Holy Church of America. He is a member of the Board of Directors of the Intercollegiate Pentecostal Conference International, the Society for Pentecostal Studies, and the Interview Panel, Protestant Fund for Theological Education. Dr. Forbes is a graduate of Howard University, Washington, D.C.; Union Theological Seminary, New York, New York; and Colgate-Rochester Divinity School, Rochester, New York, where he received his Doctor of Ministry degree. He also holds a certificate in clinical pastoral education from the Medical College of Virginia, Richmond, Virginia. He is a former pastor and campus minister. In 1973 he became the first black clergy since the Reconstruction to offer the opening prayer at the Session of the House of Delegates of the General Assembly of the Commonwealth of Virginia.

O little town of Bethlehem, how still we see thee lie!
Above thy deep and dreamless sleep the silent stars go by.
Yet in thy dark streets shineth the everlasting light;
The hopes and fears of all the years are met in thee tonight.

I thought as I read it more closely, *As I've celebrated Christmas through the years and shared in the singing of this hymn, how prosaic of me not to have noticed what a great battle must have been raging if the hopes and fears of all the years met in a small town like Bethlehem!* What a battle! All the hopes and all the fears from all the years getting together in the same territory, in that little town? What a battle! I call it the Battle of Bethlehem. And if, in the joyous mood of the Christmas season, we happen to overlook this battle, the chances are we will miss something of the cosmic significance of the Babe of Bethlehem, whom I choose to call the Hero of the Battle of Bethlehem. People like the great preacher, Phillips Brooks, make us aware of the battle so that we can really appreciate this hero sent to earth to dwell among men and women.

Christmas is about more than a little baby born in Bethlehem. It is about a battle of cosmic significance. It focuses, for us Christians, on the action in the city of David, but it is linked with the action in any city where hopes and fears compete for territory, for hearts and minds, in communities and nations where men and women seek to decide, "Which way shall I lean? Toward my hopes or toward my fears?"

Now everywhere I've been where Christmas was underway, I have suspected that people were not inclined to pay attention to the distant beat of the drum or the sound of ammunition pounding; they tended to do all they could to keep the battle dimension from entering into the Christmas celebration. Are we trying to cover up? Are we trying to ignore the battle? If not, then explain to me the profusion of booze during the season. Or the manufactured merriment, or the straining at cheerfulness and charity.

Some people never manage to buy into that. Some insist on facing the reality of the battle that rages within them. How we lament the fact that during this season while we whoop it up and live it up, people are ending their lives, refusing to be anesthetized by manufactured aesthetics of joy and peace and excitement. During these days of December, even when the twenty-fifth finally arrives, there are still people who are deciding that they're not going to play the game and, therefore, either break up, crack up, or hang it up. They know about the battle but are not yet prepared to hear about its hero.

Even those who have learned through the years to bring a sober dimension to their celebration of Christmas have to say, "Yes, Brooks, you're right." It's not only hopes that are walking around at Christmastime but fears as well. The hopes and fears of all the year and of all the years come out and start competing not only in the dark streets of Bethlehem but everywhere we go.

I hope you share my addition, through the inspiration of Phillips Brooks, to the list of battles. I want to have you look with me at what the Battle of Bethlehem must have been like, what it might be even now. Let's look at the battle between hopes and fears in Bethlehem that first Christmas night.

Will you accept some images from that first Christmas, images of the hopes in juxtaposition with the fears? First of all, the crowd. They went to Bethlehem for a census of the empire. The crowds thronged the city of Bethlehem to be counted. That's on the hope side because *to be counted* at least opens up the possibility of *being accounted for*. (Down in the South where I come from, one of the worst things you can say about a person is, "He ain't no 'count." Not to be counted means the world might just as well go on without you. It means you don't make a blip on the radar of human experience.) The crowd hoped that in complying with the order to be counted, perhaps their lot in life would improve.

And yet there were also fears that the census had no such intention. Some foreign power dominating their culture had decreed that they be counted. The crowd must have wondered, "Will they count us in order to contain us more effectively? Will it mean they will know how many garrisons need to be placed where?" The great emperor, Caesar Augustus, not having time to be concerned about what the little folk in the streets of Bethlehem were concerned about, became an agent of their fears. The people were afraid that through the act of being counted they would more likely become a zero in the cultures of the world.

Mary and Joseph were in the crowd as well. Both were decent people with significant family roots. They were people who were held in high esteem. Their hope was that somehow, through all the changes that had occurred in the recent days, they would be able to maintain a sense of self-worth. It was not enough for them to know of their own integrity. They wanted others to know that their reputation was high, that they were of solid character beneath their reputation.

And yet, Joseph and Mary—in their own ways—were not sure whether their integrity would be called in question and their reputation tarnished. "Will folks understand? Will they know that what is done is of God? What will they think of us now?" and "What will they think of my judgment in bringing Mary here to this place under these circumstances?" Both of them held high their hopes to be known as virtuous people, and yet they feared that what was happening was going to do them in, to expose them for the frailty of their flesh.

The Wise Men from the East were there. They came bearing instruments of hope and devotion. They were certain that their calculations had led them at the right time to the right general area, but as they approached the city, their hearts began to beat faster. They hoped that at long last they could vindicate their professional judgment and complete their quest, find the place and the cause where they could put all that was worthy before the One whom they considered to be the highest of all human aspirations.

And yet, their fears played havoc with them as well. They lost the trail; they were not sure. As they inquired of their professional peers in Herod's court, they were afraid their journey would be exposed as a fool's errand, that they would be embarrassed by their colleagues. They wondered if the fears they had felt at the beginning of their quest might come true: There is no place. And there is no king. And there is no credibility to the whole scheme; it was only a pipe-dream. And they must return bearing gold, frankincense, and myrrh ungiven, not having found the place in which the presents might with honor be laid before the king they hoped had been born.

And let's not leave out Herod. Herod was also there between the hopes and the fears. (I want to include him because we Christian people have a way of ignoring the hopes of other folks. We assume that we are the only ones worthy of engaging in the battle between hopes and fears!) Herod hoped to maintain the security of his present position. He hoped to maintain his power. He thought he had ruled well, considering the political situation. He had not anticipated any kind of coup d'etat, did not feel he deserved it. But here come the Wise Men, asking, "Where is he who is going to be the king of the Jews?" So he had his fears as well, "What is this threat? Perhaps I am going to be displaced or replaced. Maybe I'm going to be upstaged, phased out; and if this threat is not nipped in the bud now, it might live to haunt me later."

And there were shepherds also, abiding in the field. They were hoping that the flock would turn out well, that they could eke out a bare existence for their families. And I suspect that occasionally they hoped that when they started to tell a story, as they sat beneath the stars, they would not hear, "Oh, you told that story last year." They hoped something new would happen so that they could say, "Look, I've got a new one tonight!" As they gathered their sheep about them, they hoped that there was something new in the universe. They hoped that novelty had not been barricaded in the past. They hoped for something to uplift them, to give them a new story to tell as they scraped their pittance from the soil and watched over their flocks.

And yet they had fears: "Nothing new is ever going to happen around here. And if something new *does* happen, it's surely going to shatter us." So that night in Bethlehem, even when the angel of the Lord *did* come and the light *did* shine round about them, they were *afraid* that this new thing had come to destroy them. Yet the angel said, "Fear not: for, behold, I bring you good tidings of great joy, which shall be to all people" (Luke 2:10).

Oh, little town of Bethlehem, the hopes and fears of all the years are met in you tonight. We don't need much time to make the transition from the first Bethlehem and its battle to the Bethlehem of our time. For do we not also share the sense that the hopes and fears of ancient Bethlehem are still at work in Bethlehem today? We saw it on television—the reporters telling us how the crowds thronged through the streets of Bethlehem, how soldiers patrolled lest guerrillas attack and mar this sacred holiday. We saw it on TV—how shopkeepers asked the soldiers, "Would you please take off your guns when you come into this shop?"

Yes, the battle of hopes and fears goes on even now, not only in Bethlehem but in every city whether it's a little city or an urban metropolis. Hopes and fears at Christmastime don't go underground. The battle goes on. And I think we all can say in our hearts, "Yes, Phillips Brooks, you are right: 'the hopes and fears of all the years are met in thee tonight.' "

For isn't it true that we all want to count? We all want our interests to be taken seriously in the universe. That's true for Jews, and it's true for Arabs as well. It's true for blacks, and it's true for whites as well. It's true for rich; it's true for poor. It's true for the folks who feel they must develop defense and for the folks who feel they must fight for peace. It's true for conservatives as well as liberals. We all want to count. We may call each other "No-'count," but in that very process we acknowledge that the other wants to count. And we fear that *we* will not count.

Yet isn't it true that we all want honor? Which one of us really enjoys being called a rascal? We all wish for the honor of a good reputation; we want our character to be untarnished. We want the Good Housekeeping Seal of Moral Rectitude from our families and our communities. But the sins that lurk in our hearts will do us in; like termites they will rot away the foundation of our existence. We will be exposed to the time of the great swarming.

We all search for a place of ultimate worth; we'd like to find a job where we can give everything we've got. We'd like to find a cause that's untarnished, a cause we can give ourselves to unreservedly. We all have a goal; we're all on a quest; and we want to get to the place where we can celebrate, "This is the place where all that I am is called forth in devotion and honor." Who is it among us who is not without a sense of vocational uncertainty? Working harder, but with a diminished sense of satisfaction? Asking if what we're doing is really worth the energy we put in it? Is there anybody, for example, who is not a little bit like Herod? Anybody here who isn't a little bit worried about whether his or her security will be maintained in the next decade? Aren't you scared about the erosion of your power? Aren't you afraid about the encroachment on your strength and your reserve for life? I think even now the hopes and fears of all the years meet on Christmas.

And yet, there's a hero. The battle's for real. And we ought to stop hiding our heads and pretending it's a great, big, joyous holiday. We ought to stop talking about Christmas as a time when light finally breaks through the darkness and all is right with the world. The battle continues to rage. It was raging the day before Christmas, and it's going on even now. And yet, the reason we can afford to take out time to celebrate is because there's a hero. There is One who has come in the form of a baby, who is God's signal that we don't fight the battle alone. The Babe of Bethlehem became the Hero of Bethlehem. But that took time to develop into a faith affirmation.

Why don't we Christians acknowledge that not all of what we affirm about Christmas was evident on that first night? It took years for us finally to come to understand—as we walked and moved in the living presence of Christ, as we heard the news of his resurrection, as we saw him go forth and declare that he would send us his spirit—that it is in the light of continuous walking with the Babe that we now go back to tell the story with all the richness we can muster about this Hero.

I call him "my hero." I want to tell you why. First of all, in that battle raging between hopes and fears in Bethlehem, Jesus came, a little baby, but he arranged a cease-fire. In the midst of our battling with hopes and fears, we all need from time to time to have a cease-fire. You can't fight all the time; your energy runs out. You cannot sustain the offensive all the time without going back to the depot and renewing yourself. Jesus becomes the hallowed and holy center that calls us away from the battle to worship.

I like to think that a worship service, among other things, is a cease-fire. It is a time to put the guns down. It is a time to say to the enemy, "Wait a minute now. I have to go to church; I've heard that the Christ child is born, and I want to go and adore him." It is the hero who arranges the cease-fire to allow us to come and sit and think about the promises made known through all ancient Israel, to talk about God's intentions for this created order, to come and hear that God has not lost faith but has continued to give to those who wait in expectation. So Jesus' birth calls us to worship, arranges a cease-fire. Put yourselves at rest now. The battle rages, and in just a little while we've got to go back out there. But rest a while. Relax. God hath not abandoned us. God is in the midst of us; God will help us; God tells us to have confidence.

We are not urged to overlook the battle. It is real. But every now and then, you have to be still. I know the battle rages in your homes; be still. I know there's conflict in some minds represented in this congregation this morning; but be still. I know some of you are involved in causes that are being set back now; but just for a little while, be still. The Hero has arranged a cease-fire. Look and look well, for the promise of his appearance on the earth will be kept. This is the witness of all those who walked with him and talked with him, and I'm inclined to join it, too. Let's be still. He has arranged for us a cease-fire.

God tells us through Jesus Christ, "Look. You know that little conflict in your heart and mind? You know the trouble you've had at your home? You know the difficulty we're facing in our cities? You know all the conflict in the world today? Don't distort it; that's just a part of the larger battle." So the coming of the Hero of Bethlehem is to let us know that, yes, the battle between hopes and fears goes on.

But don't be deceived; there's a greater battle. Jesus Christ makes it known, as we continue to walk with him, that the battle is between the kingdom of God and the kingdoms of the world, that the battle involves cosmic consequences. God has something in mind, but institutions and systems have something else in mind. Principalities and powers at the core of the universe are locked in battle, and your little battle, your little conflict, is just one of the skirmishes in this great battle.

Christmas is a time when all our strivings are put in a larger context. Jesus makes it very clear that there are many battlefields; your mind is one of them, and your heart may be one of them. Sometimes even your church may become one of them. But the forces are the same, conflict between these two kingdoms, going on and on. And even after you get your little problem solved, don't forget that the battle rages on, and you'll find it at some other place as well.

The battle is waged, but your Lord and mine comes and reveals the strategy saying, "There's a cosmic battle going on, and your little problems and conflicts are a part of that battle. We will take them as some of the early engagements, guerrilla warfare, if you will." He reveals a strategy. Let me tell you what I hear him saying, "Now listen. Hopes and fears are locked in deadly array. But I am the bearer of a plan, a plan based on love, power, justice, peace, and truth." He says, "I have come to demonstrate the folly and futility of fear. I have come to expose the flaws in the fabric of the world's system. I have come—just like another man who came from Bethlehem, little David, and fought the giant—to face the giant called Death and Destruction on behalf of all of us. When I have demonstrated who I am, how I am the bearer of the victory in the midst of the struggle between hopes and fears, I'm going to turn around and recruit some of you and equip you also to be agents of the kingdom. I'm going to recruit some of you to be truth-tellers, peacemakers, justice-shapers, power-bearers, and love-spreaders—that's what I'm going to do."

Oh, little town of Bethlehem, the hopes and fears of all the years are met in you tonight. But, thank God, there's a Hero who has made it clear that he is with us, *Emmanuel,* to enable us to stand fast in the midst of the battles of life. Well, brothers and sisters, I want to ask you a question now, Is there anything I have said that speaks to you? Have you ever experienced Jesus as the Hero of Bethlehem coming to you as you were stretched out between the hopes and fears, to help you to move toward the hopes? For if Jesus is with us, in the midst of our struggles, he gives us perspective and vision. If Jesus is with us, he sustains our energy for the engagement. If Jesus comes and leans with us on the hope side, we can find encouragement to be alert for creative possibilities in the places where we struggle. If Jesus is with us, he sides with the hope dimension of the battle and calls us to celebrate even while we face perplexing reality.

When I was writing this sermon, it was as if Jesus came to me and said, "You're talking about me as the Hero of Bethlehem. Jim, what do I mean to *you*? Not what shall you preach to the people—what do I mean to you?" And I found myself answering him, "Jesus, I'm not just preaching about you. You're my ideal. I don't know anybody in the world or beyond the world who challenges me as you do. Jesus, I'm impressed with your integrity. I am impressed with your power, your vision, your love, your peace, your discipline, your courage, your faithfulness; and in the moments when I'm not watching myself, I find myself thinking, 'To be like Jesus—oh, how I long to be like him!' "

I said, "Jesus, not only are you my ideal, but you are my deliverer. There have been so many times when in the midst of my struggles between hope and fear you've come to me and released me from my guilt about things that I have done. You've come to me, and you've lifted me—how many times!—out of depression. You've helped me overcome long periods of meaninglessness, and when I'm scared, you come to me and say, 'Be not afraid; lo, I am with you.' "

I said to Jesus, "Jesus, not only are you my ideal, not only are you my deliverer, but you're my Lord. I'm willing to bet my life that you are Lord of history—that the way the whole, created scheme of things turns out will hinge on what you do. Jesus, you're my Lord because I'm willing to take my cues from you. I'm willing to take orders from you. I'm willing to receive encouragement from you. I'm willing to participate with you in this cosmic battle between the kingdoms. Jesus, I have confidence in you; my hope rests in you. You are my hero; you are my leader. And I'm going to stick with you."

Christmas is going to leave us behind. But if Jesus goes ahead of us, if Jesus leads us, we'll make it all right. The world is like a mine field, and destructive possibilities rest everywhere; but if we can keep our eyes on him, following a fellowship where Jesus is also the hero, testing our actions in the world by his standards, then the year that lies ahead will be a different year because we have contacted the Hero of Bethlehem. Oh, little town of Bethlehem, the hopes and fears of all the years are met in you tonight, but there's also a Hero here. And his name is Jesus. And if he is here, we shall sing, while the eternal ages roll, about hope triumphing over fear.

Let us pray. O Lord God, here we are with our hopes and fears. Grant that out of our Christmas celebration some gift of insight might come so that, having affirmed Jesus as Lord, we may go forth with confidence and hope. Through his name we pray, and in his power we live. Amen. ○

How Far Is the Promised Land?

Leonard Lovett

Deuteronomy 34:1-4

Introduction

By faith as a people we have come out of Egypt and even crossed the Red Sea, but the promise lies ahead. We have also received a majority report that it is indeed a fertile land, a land flowing with milk and honey. The land is also strongly fortified. The inhabitants are so large in size, we appeared like grasshoppers to them. There are indeed giants even in the land of promise. The minority report: With all of the above, God makes the difference. Both reports are factual.

The parallels between the lives of Moses and Martin Luther King,

Dr. Leonard Lovett is the pastor of the Church at the Crossroads, Los Angeles, California, and the associate director of black studies, Fuller Theological Seminary, Pasadena, California. He is a member of the American Academy of Religion, the Society for the Study of Black Religion, the National Black Evangelical Association, and the Society for Pentecostal Studies. He has been a contributor to several religious publications, such as *Logos, Pentecostal World,* and *The Journal of the Interdenominational Theological Center*. Dr. Lovett is a graduate of Morehouse College, Atlanta, Georgia; Crozer Theological Seminary, Chester, Pennsylvania; and Emory University, Atlanta, Georgia, where he received his Ph.D.

Jr., are indeed striking; the connection of faith makes the comparison meaningful.

1. Jehovah gave Moses an honorable title: Moses, the servant of God.

    History has accorded King the title, "the Peaceful Warrior".

2. Moses forsook a princedom in Egypt and chose to suffer affliction with the people of God.

    King bypassed several college presidencies, remained a resident of the ghetto, and was assassinated while supporting garbage workers in Memphis, Tennessee.

3. Moses faced his death with courage and confidence.

    King retorted on the evening of his death, "I would like to live a long life. I'm not fearing any man, but mine eyes have seen the glory of the Lord."

4. Moses succumbed at a time when Israel was poised for attack with the land of promise within reach.

    King was assassinated at a time when he was shifting his tactics with his call for massive civil disobedience campaigns; but his strategy (commitment to nonviolent resistance) remained.

5. Moses died in the fullness of strength.

    King was slain in the prime of his life at age thirty-nine.

6. Moses was carried to the top of Pisgah, also called Mt. Nebo.

    King proclaimed: "I've been to the mountaintop. I've looked over."

7. Moses had received advanced notice that he would not be entering the Promised Land.

    King was doubtful whether he would be physically present to enter the Promised Land.

1. The Promised Land

To wanderers and nomads, used to life in the barren wilderness, Canaan was a veritable paradise. Let's take a brief journey on the pinions of faith and on the wings of imagination to the solitude of Mt. Pisgah with Moses as he views the land promised to his fathers. We find him basking in the sunlight of a prophet's wish, near the stars, alone. Only the silence of nature is his companion, for it is in the absence of the noise of earth that one can realize the nearness of the invisible Spirit and begin to reflect on the sublime majesty of God. Here stands Moses, alone on the brow of the mountain with the view of Canaan at his feet. Mountains have often been selected by God as the scene of grand divine events. On the summit of a mountain we are inspired with a sense of awe and reverence. We are constrained to worship as we absorb the sense of the infinite.

The panorama of a mighty landscape comes into view. To the north lies Gilead and the mountain plateau divided by the ford of Jabbock with rocky plains, hill pastures, forests of oak and pine. Beyond Gennesaret he can see the wild land on both sides of the Jordan and Mt. Hermon with its peaks crowned by eternal snows; the green cedars of Lebanon wave their branches in the distance. As Moses shifts his gaze towards the Great Sea, the fertile cornfields of Esdraelon come into sight; them Moses looks at the rugged Mt. Carmel where Elijah will later mock the worshipers of Canaanite gods by reminding them that perhaps Baal is on vacation. Then comes the broken highlands where Ephraim would soon crouch like a lion in his den; Moses looks westward where he sees the plain of Judah; right below at his feet lies the Dead Sea with its surrounding crater-cup of hills. He sees Jericho with its verdant green pastures and the mountain pass that led to the hill that mankind for generations would call Zion.

This was the land Moses had yearned to possess. He must have thought about the dark days in Egypt with God's oppressed people. He must have reflected on his calling in the backside of a desert where bushes burned and men had to take off their shoes in the presence of a holy God. The words of that theophanic experience must have replayed themselves through Moses' consciousness. He must have heard the repetition of that voice saying, "Moses, I've got some people in bondage, and I want you to speak to Pharoah and tell him to let my people go. If he questions your credentials, tell him 'I am' sent you." Finite man must say, "I am that I am because of my status, and so forth." God says, "I am that I am," period. He must have remembered God's silencing the tongues of dogs as the death angel passed through Egypt on the night of deliverance, how God led the people by a pillar of fire by night and a luminous cloud by day. And he perhaps recalled how God scooped out a highway through the Red Sea as the waters congealed like jelly.

In retrospect, he must have thought about the forty year sojourn in the wilderness—manna from on high, tables of necessity, how they marched and counter-marched as God prepared them for a future yet to be. His heart must have lurched forward and beat faster as he thought about what it would be like to set foot in the land of promise.

All of a sudden, Moses' world became tarnished by the black paint of pessimism. He made a final plea to enter the Promised Land, but the Eternal God answered no. The narrative ends with the death of the servant of the Lord on the summit of Mt. Pisgah in full view of the land of promise.

No promise, vision, or dream whose source is the Eternal God dissipates because the visionary leader dies. The dream in this instance is spiritual. Consequently, it became reincarnated in another dreamer in a different place at another time. Like atoms spiritual dreams rearrange themselves within the consciousness of another dreamer.

Joshua and Caleb entered the divine scenario by leading a conquest into Canaan. They planned military strategy under the guidance of the captain of the Lord's host, and the walls of Jericho, the key city, came tumbling down. The giants were conquered. With the presence of the Eternal God who takes off chariot wheels in order to defeat enemies who attempt to thwart his purposes, we shall overcome.

Many centuries later, there lived a people who knew something about ancient dusty rivers. There lived a people whose revered homeland was the continent of Africa. Physically linked together in captivity, men, women, and children were uprooted from their homeland by colonial slave traders and were transported by way of the Middle Passage to a place called the New World. The New World was a harrowing nightmare place where millions of slaves died from disease, hunger strikes, and even suicide. According to some of the lower estimates, more than thirteen and a half million slaves were imported to North America, South America, and the West Indies during the slave trading era.

Because slave labor was cheap, the New World became a veritable hell for slaves, a kind of Egypt. In an alien land, they felt the searing pain of the master's whip laying bare the tissues of human flesh; they watched friends being mutilated, families divided, others choosing to commit suicide rather than accept a fate consigned to them by their masters. In the midst of their suffering they also experienced the presence of the Eternal God. He was not Paul Tillich's "Ground of Being" or Hegel's "Absolute Spirit" but a battle-ax in the time of trouble, a shelter in the time of storm. It is often within oppressive situations that we can realize divine presence.

As slaves worked in the cotton fields of the South, hope was born. As they worked, they composed songs, "sorrow songs," out of their environment. With eyes of faith, slaves could look beyond their immediate enslavement and translate hope out of their existential situation. As they saw the slave master approaching in a horse-drawn carriage, they reasoned, *One day God is going to send down a chariot for us*. So they sang "Swing Low." When they looked at the master's shoes, they sang within, "I've got shoes, you got. . . ." Or the master would teach them to read the Bible, usually beginning with such a passage as "Servants, obey your master. . . ." But under the unction of the Spirit, these trembling singers would find their way over to Jeremiah's question, "Is there a balm in Gilead?" They would translate this question into an affirmation, "There is a balm. . . ."

Before 1800 the dream of freedom became reincarnated in such personalities as Prince Hall, Benjamin Banneker, and Richard Allen, and they solidly denounced slavery as inhumane.

In 1800 Gabriel Prosser, Denmark Vesey, and Nat Turner rebelled against slavery.

In 1827 Samuel Cornish and John Russwurm initiated the first black newspaper, called "Freedom's Journal," which demanded the end of slavery.

In 1829 Robert Young published his Ethiopian Manifesto prediction that a black liberator would someday arise and lead his people to freedom. The *dream of freedom* became reincarnated in David Walker, and he wrote his *Appeal,* calling upon the slaves to rise up in revolution against their bondage. The *dream of freedom* invaded Sojourner Truth's mind, and she journeyed throughout the land, crying out for justice. Henry Ward, Henry Highland Garnett, and Frederick Douglas, who so eloquently reminded us that no freedom comes without struggle, also had the *dream of freedom*. The *dream of freedom* motivated William Lloyd Garrison, who through his militant journal, "The Liberator," became the most outstanding white spokesman for militant abolition.

The *dream of freedom* became reincarnated in Harriet Tubman who became legitimated as the slaves' hero in her bold stand against slavery as she conducted several hundred persons to freedom by way of the underground railroad. As a slave girl, she was called Minti. After she defied the system, they called her Harriet. After she led her people to the Promised Land of the North, she was revered and called "Moses" by her people. They knew when she was near because she would hoot like an owl and whistle like a whippoorwill or sing the "Chariot's Coming". When the slave masters asked, "Who is this man, Moses?" the slaves smiled to themselves, *Our Moses is a woman*. After some nineteen trips, Harriet was asked where she got her courage. Reaching into her bosom, she whipped out a well-worn Bible and read Luke 4:18, "The Spirit of the Lord is upon me. . . ."

Then came Lincoln's "Emancipation Proclamation" and reconstruction in our national history. With forty acres and a mule, some slaves thought the Promised Land had arrived. As a people, we have learned through the midnight of oppression to hold fast to our dreams.

For in that long line of visionaries came Martin Luther King, Jr. Born during the beginning of a severe depression in the thirties, his heart and mind were trained in the forties at Morehouse College and Crozer Theological Seminary, preparing for the momentous fifties. From Gandhi, King appropriated the method of nonviolent resistance, but from Jesus, he received the motivation of love. From personalism he learned something about the sacredness of human personality, the dignity and worth of the individual before God. That is why he attacked segregation as a monstrous evil that would eventually destroy the segregators as well as the segregated, for the same barriers you erect for others will eventually become prison bars to your own soul. From the black religious experience he learned that God takes sides with the oppressed and even fights for them.

From Montgomery to Memphis he preached, prayed, planned, and strategized. His sermon style and sayings often reflected George F. Hegel's dialectics (thesis—antithesis—synthesis). That is why he was at home as he talked about a transformed nonconformist or a tough mind and a tender heart: "Shattered Dreams," "Death of Evil Upon the Seashore," "Love In Action," "Loving Your Enemies," "Pilgrimage to Non-Violence," and "Letter from a Birmingham Jail."

We often attribute the integrationist thrust of the Black Revolution to King. I believe it was initiated when a black woman named Rosa Park was enroute home. She had traveled that same route many times, perhaps with the same driver. But December 5, 1955, was destined to be a different day in history. When the bus driver asked Rosa Parks to move to the rear and give up her seat for whites, her refusal was not even an ordinary one. In the words of King, "She was not planted there by the NAACP or any other organization; she was planted there by her personal sense of dignity and self-respect." So she was anchored to that seat by the accumulated indignity of days gone by and the boundless aspirations of generations yet unborn. She was a victim of both the forces of history and the forces of destiny. She had been tracked down by the Zeitgeist, "the spirit of the time." This event set in motion this momentous phase of the black struggle, and King was called in to provide leadership.

After the victory in Montgomery, King came to Atlanta during the beginning of the decade of the sixties when students throughout the South were sitting in until men and women stood up in dignity. He was there when students marched with Klansmen on one side of the road and students on the other, walking, talking, and protesting in dignity. I was a junior at Morehouse College when King arrived. I remember the urgent admonitions to all of us to remain nonviolent regardless of what happened as we marched.

In a world that is violence-prone, we need to listen once again to the wisdom of this social prophet who lived among us. In one of his first articles he stated that the purpose of the Montgomery boycott was reconciliation, the end was redemption, the goal was the creation of the beloved community. He further reminded us that "the most creative turn of events in man's long history occurred when man gave up his stone axe and began to cooperate with his neighbor." In order to achieve the beloved community, our loyalties must transcend our race, tribe, class, and our nation. He believed with all his heart that this would lead inevitably to a completely integrated society, a community of love and justice. To King this would be the ideal corporate expression of the faith.

King's idealism was kept in check by his realism. King was acutely aware that the kingdom of God is "not yet" a reality and that there are many obstacles to overcome. He admitted that "while the Kingdom may remain 'not yet' as a universal reality in history, in the present it may exist in such isolated forms as in judgment, in personal devotion and in group life." The rule and reign of God is both present and future. The kingdom is present and is also in the process of becoming. It comes in isolated forms as liberation among humankind. It comes in part when oppressive regimes, such as Idi Amin's, crumble. It comes in part when we are brought to our senses by the enigmas of a Watergate experience.

Martin is no longer with us. He now belongs to the ages. In April,

1968, Martin, like Moses, left us on the summit of the mountaintop. Martin left us on the summit of future expectations, on the tableland of a future yet to be and still in the process of becoming. With strained vision and flowing adrenalin we must ask, "How far is the promised land?" When we are reminded by educators and social scientists that there are more segregated schools in this nation than there were fifteen or twenty years ago, we must ask, how far is the Promised Land?

The Promised Land is as far away as our unwillingness to work seriously at genuine intergroup and interpersonal living. If we are to reach the Promised Land, blacks, Hispanics, Asians, and all oppressed peoples must work harder at participation in coalition politics.

The Promised Land is as far away as our refusal to recognize that the choice is no longer that of violence or nonviolence but it is, to use the words of King, "nonviolence or nonexistence."

The Promised Land is as far away as our unwillingness to expose and end the sophisticated forms of discrimination against minorities, the subtle forms of institutionalized racism that destroy the social fabric of our society.

The Promised Land is as far away as this nation's unwillingness to understand what real violence is. Violence occurs when farmers are paid not to farm while poor people go undernourished for lack of basics. Violence occurs when 50 percent of a national budget goes for defense (death rather than life). Violence occurs when the mass media are used to perpetuate stereotypes. Violence occurs when oppressed children sleep in rat-infested traps that go unnoticed because of greedy absentee landlords.

How far is the Promised Land?

It is as close as minorities getting themselves together spiritually, educationally, and politically so that we can equally participate in the decision-making areas of this society.

It is as close as our ability to move against the wholesale misuse of dangerous drugs that destroy our best minds before they can fulfill their potential.

It is as close as our faith that truth will ultimately triumph over evil.

It is as close as minorities realizing that we must begin in our own communities to stop killing one another and ripping off one another.

It is as close as our willingness to stop buying the false images of idols and gods of Hollywood and create our own role models.

It is as close as our realization that as blacks in America we are still holding a bad check in our hands marked insufficient funds because this nation has defaulted and refused to honor it at the Bank of Justice.

Since the kingdom of this world has not become the kingdom of our Lord and of his Christ, we must move forward. As we plunge forward into the eighties, we must not allow our forward progress to be stymied by broken promises, unfulfilled dreams, withering aspirations, moral ambiguities and contradictions, the shadow of war, and shattered hopes. ○

Thanksgiving

Benjamin E. Mays

This is the Thanksgiving season, and we are justified in raising the following question with hope, faith, skepticism, and pessimism, "What have we to be thankful for?"

Many of you know the history of Thanksgiving in the United States. But before pointing out to you what we have to be thankful for at the end of 1981, let me give you the history of Thanksgiving in the United States.

Thanksgiving is a day set apart on which to give thanks for the blessings of the year. It was suggested, no doubt, by the English

Dr. Benjamin E. Mays is the president emeritus, Morehouse College, Atlanta, Georgia, where he served as president from 1940 to 1967. Dr. Mays is a graduate of Bates College, Lewiston, Maine, and the University of Chicago, Chicago, Illinois, where he received his Ph.D. He is the recipient of numerous honorary degrees from institutions of higher education, such as the University of Liberia, the Interdenominational Theological Center, and Boston University. From 1921 to 1924 he pastored the Shiloh Baptist Church, Atlanta, Georgia. He has served as the dean of the School of Religion, Howard University, president of the United Negro College Fund, and as a member of the National Advisory Council to the Peace Corps. Dr. Mays is the author of *The Negro's Church, The Negro's God, Seeking to Be Christian in Race Relations, Disturbed About Man,* and *Born to Rebel.*

Harvest Home, an old-fashioned festival held to celebrate the completion of harvest. A similar festival in Scotland was known as Mell Supper.

The first American Thanksgiving Day was observed by Plymouth Colony on November 26, 1621. The observance of the day became general throughout New England. After the Revolutionary War the celebration of Thanksgiving spread to the middle states and over the west, making progress more slowly southward. The governors of most states issued Thanksgiving proclamations. Until 1939 the last Thursday in November was observed as Thanksgiving Day. President Roosevelt then requested, with a view toward stimulating business, that this national holiday be observed one week earlier. This observance was not compulsory since the governor of each state sets the date to be celebrated. In 1940 two-thirds of the states followed President Roosevelt's suggestion, and today all states observe the earlier date.

The original Plymouth Thanksgiving was held under peculiar circumstances. After the first corn crop had been gathered, Governor Bradford and the pilgrim fathers decided to have a feast of ingathering, a day of Thanksgiving.

When the pilgrims landed in Massachusetts, many of their colleagues had died on the Mayflower, and many died shortly after their arrival. By reason and logic the survivors could have cursed God; whether agnostic, infidel, atheist, or humanist, they might have cursed God and died. No, they put on a picnic and feasted. They called together the Indians and thanked God for those pilgrims who were left.

Real troubles, hard times, and death did not dampen their faith in God. It has been said that there are no atheists in fox holes. We look beyond ourselves for something that we do not have—for family, friends, the country—and finally we cry out loudly saying, "O God Almighty, have mercy on me; what can I do; save us Lord." This is true of the rich and the poor, for the young and the old, for the high and the low, and the great and the small. No matter which of these we may be, we all travel the same road from our mother's womb to the grave. So there is no need for any of us to think we are better off than any other man or woman.

We can thank God that despite the world conditions we are not in a destructive war in which Russia and the United States are using atomic and hydrogen weapons of destruction to destroy each other.

Despite the fact that the administration has increased the military budget, we are not in war!! We are not in war despite the cuts in money for the aging, mounting unemployment, and cuts in the school lunch program.

The world is in a terrible condition. More than half the people of the world are living in conditions of misery. Their food is inadequate. The world bank estimates that some eight hundred million people live in absolute poverty. Life expectancy in developing countries is fifty-six years; in the industrialized countries, the life expectancy is seventy-two. One in ten infants in the developing world dies before its first birthday; in the industrial world, only one in fifty dies.

In one respect, the north-south gap has begun to narrow. Pinched by rising oil prices and inflation, the growth rate of northern industrial economies fell to 3.4 percent a year during the 1970s while that of the developing south grew at a rate of 5.7 percent. Even so, the thirty-five poorest nations, the home of 1.1 billion people, one-fourth of the world's population, were left further behind with per capita incomes of less than three hundred dollars per year and a wretched 3 percent slice of the world's wealth.

In light of this grave situation President Reagan is insisting on cutting the school lunch programs and food stamp programs, throwing heavy burdens on the states to pick up the tab amounting to fifty to seventy billion dollars in taxes, while expecting to spend three trillion dollars on defense within the next few years. School boards all over the country are protesting this three trillion dollars for atomic and hydrogen weapons of war.

After twenty years in public life, I join most Americans in getting my 'briefings' from the morning paper and the evening news. In watching events in the nation and the world unfold and trying my best to understand and interpret, I am ever conscious of our nation's strength and resilience and ability to solve problems. I relish the opportunity to participate in this process, and I intend to do so with everything that's in me.

What can we do in these troubled times? We can rely on the Bible for religious, moral, and ethical support and values which our nation has never considered.

Moses led the Israelites out of Egypt. He spent forty years wandering around in the wilderness trying to lead his fellow men who wanted to go back to Egypt rather than fight for freedom.

How strange!! How modern! These pilgrims standing for freedom in their own land. It takes a long time to emancipate an enslaved people. We black people should know this. Unfortunately, nations have never relied on religious, moral, and ethical power.

> When the Son of man shall come in his glory, and all the holy angels with him, then shall he sit upon the throne of his glory: And before him shall be gathered all nations: and he shall separate them one from another, as a shepherd divideth his sheep from the goats: and he shall set the sheep on his right hand, but the goats on the left. Then shall the King say unto them on his right hand, Come, ye blessed of my Father, inherit the kingdom prepared for you from the foundation of the world: for I was an hungred, and ye gave me meat: I was thirsty, and ye gave me drink: I was a stranger, and ye took me in: Naked, and ye clothed me: I was sick, and ye visited me: I was in prison, and ye came unto me. Then shall the righteous answer him, saying, Lord, when saw we thee an hungred, and fed thee? or thirsty, and gave thee drink? When saw we thee a stranger, and took thee in? or naked, and clothed thee? Or when saw we thee sick, or in prison, and came unto thee? And the King shall answer and say unto them, Verily I say unto you, Inasmuch as ye have done it unto one of the least of these my brethren, ye have done it unto me. Then shall he say also unto them on the left hand, Depart from me, ye cursed, into everlasting fire, prepared for the devil and his angels: For I was an hungred, and ye gave me no meat: I was thirsty, and ye gave me no drink: I was a stranger, and ye took me not in: naked, and ye clothed me not: sick, and in prison, and ye visited me not. Then shall they also answer him, saying, Lord, when saw we thee an hungred, or athirst, or a stranger, or naked, or sick, or in prison, and did not minister unto thee? Then shall he answer them, saying, Verily I say unto you, Inasmuch as ye did it not to one of the least of these, ye did it not to me. And these shall go away into everlasting punishment: but the righteous into life eternal" (Matthew 25:31-46).

What can we, as blacks, do? It may be that God has called upon black people, black Americans to be a special people. It is my belief, it is my firm conviction, that God has sent every man and every woman into the world to do something unique, something distinctive, and that if he or she does not do it, it will never be done and the world will be the loser. The call to do this unique thing does not go to the crowd or to the multitude but to the individual or a specific nation—mainly to a particular person and often a particular race. Yes, I do believe that God has sent every man and every woman into the world to do something unique and something distinctive, and if he or she does not do it, it will never be done.

What can we be thankful for? We can be thankful that the early Christians resisted the brutal murders of the Neroes, the Caesars, the

Domitians, and other cruel emperors. Many of the Christians died by allowing their bodies to be thrown to the wild beasts in the arena rather than accept the emperor's beliefs in the Roman gods. We can be thankful for these believing Christians who died a long time ago, dying for their faith in their God. We can thank God who helped the Jews to establish a new nation. Yes, we can thank God for Amos and Hosea, Micah and Malachi, Isaiah and Jeremiah, Habakkuk and Ezekiel who suffered for their faith without which we would have died in despair.

If the churches of the north had not come down at the close of the Civil War to educate the newly emancipated slaves, no other church group would have done it. These people came into the south for no other purpose than to develop and emancipate the minds of black Americans. They didn't come for money, they didn't come for wealth, and they didn't come for prestige; they came only to teach the newly emancipated people.

The Baptists came and established Shaw, Morehouse, Bishop, and Benedict.

The Congregationalists came south and established Atlanta University, Fisk, Talladega, and what is now Dillard University.

The United Methodists came south and established Clark, Bennett, and Wiley.

If these denominations had not come south after the Civil War, the black man would not have been taught. They had to break up the segregation in God's house. Someday history should be written to give the churches credit and to thank God that segregation was broken up in the house of the Lord. We can be thankful for that.

We can be thankful for William Lloyd Garrison and Harriett Beecher Stowe, whom Lincoln honored by saying her *Uncle Tom's Cabin* precipitated the Civil War. In the Thanksgiving season we can thank God for these.

We can thank God for Frederick Douglass, who ran away from slavery. He ran away from his master to be a free man, and he became a greater emancipator than Henry Ward Beecher, for Douglass went to Europe and carried the message of slavery to the people of Europe and was proclaimed everywhere as the greatest orator in the world. We can thank God for Frederick Douglass.

We can thank God for Harriet Tubman, who by the way of the underground railroad carried three hundred Negroes to Canada to freedom's land. We can thank God for Harriet Tubman.

We can thank God for W. E. B. Dubois, who graduated from Fisk and Harvard University and, if he had been white, could have been a professor at Harvard University. W. E. B. Dubois might have easily passed as a foreigner, but he left Great Barrington, Massachusetts, went to Fisk and on to Harvard, and in 1903 wrote one of the greatest books of all times, *The Souls of Black Folks*. In this book he spoke in prophetic language and defined the problem of the twentieth century as the color line, and he spent all of his years fighting discrimination and injustice. Let us thank God for W. E. B. Dubois.

Let us thank God for Booker Washington. Without his genius there would not have been a Tuskegee Institute. It was not an accident that Booker Washington was called from Hampton to Tuskegee. When he went to Hampton, one of the white persons in charge at Hampton sent Booker Washington to clean a room, and when she went into the room to see how well Booker Washington had cleaned it, the room looked so "spic 'n span" she rubbed her handkerchief across the desk and it was as clean as if she had just brought it from the laundry. So when Tuskegee wanted a man, they sent for Booker Washington.

I used to criticize Booker Washington and Robert Russa Moton, but I have grown wiser with the years and I don't criticize Booker Washington any more. I was leaning more and more toward the Dubois philosophy. But, in the enlightenment of my old age of eighty-seven, I thank God for W. E. B. Dubois and thank God for Booker Washington. Booker Washington could not have written *Souls of Black Folks,* and W. E. B. Dubois could not have built Tuskegee Institute, and all the noise about Dubois and the Washington philosophy had no right to be.

When Robert Russa Moton took the position that Negroes should man the veterans hospital put up for Negroes who served in the wars of our country, Moton's life was threatened by the Ku Klux Klan. The Klan sent word to Moton that if he put Negroes at the head of the hospital, they would burn it down. I understand, on good authority, that Moton sent word to the Klan, "Come and burn it down. You say you love Booker Washington, and Booker Washington did more for Alabama than any other man. If you say you appreciate Booker Washington and now you want to burn the veterans hospital down, come and burn it down, and the world will know how much you loved Booker Washington." When Moton stood up like that to the Ku Klux Klan, my respect for him grew a thousand percent. Let us thank God for Robert Russa Moton.

John Hope could have passed for white in any man's world, but he elected to stay in the black race and had a great hand in building Morehouse College. We can thank God for John Hope.

We can thank God for Walter White, who could have passed for white anywhere, and yet he went around investigating lynchings and was almost lynched himself in his trade. Let us thank God for Walter White.

We thank God for Fred Patterson who brought the healing art to Tuskegee with his veterinary medicine. Let us thank God for Fred Patterson.

Let us thank God for Luther Foster who represented the State Department in several areas of the world, extending Tuskegee's information beyond the boundaries of the United States.

Finally, in closing, let us thank God for Benjamin Payton, whom God has called to walk in the path of Booker Washington, Robert Russa Moton, Fred Patterson, Luther Foster, and all of these men who have been called of God; and Benjamin Payton has been called to Tuskegee for such a time as this.

Let me close with one of my precious poems.

God's Minute

I have only just a minute,
Only sixty seconds in it,
Forced upon me—can't refuse it,
Didn't seek it, didn't choose it.
But it's up to me to use it,
I must suffer if I lose it,
Give account if I abuse it,
Just a tiny little minute—
But eternity is in it!!!

Relevant Religion

Samuel D. Proctor

I want to speak this morning on religion that is relevant for the life of the city. The eighth verse of the sixth chapter of Micah is one of the easiest verses in the Bible to remember because it has such a logical sequence to it: "He hath shewed thee, O man, what is good; and what doth the LORD require of thee but to do justly, and to love mercy, and to walk humbly with thy God?" I'm not sure that Micah meant we should put these things in a kind of stair-step order, making justice

---

Dr. Samuel D. Proctor is the pastor of the Abyssinian Baptist Church, New York, New York. He is also professor of education, Graduate School of Education (Martin Luther King Memorial Chair) Rutgers University, New Brunswick, New Jersey. He served as president of Virginia Union University (1955-1960) and North Carolina A & T State University (1960-1964). From 1964 to 1969 he held administrative positions with the Peace Corps in Nigeria and Washington, the National Council of Churches, the Office of Economic Opportunity, the Institute for Services to Education, and the University of Wisconsin.

Dr. Proctor is an alumnus of Virginia Union University, Richmond, Virginia; Crozer Theological Seminary, Chester, Pennsylvania; he earned his doctorate in ethics at Boston University, Boston, Massachusetts. He has been awarded honorary doctoral degrees by several institutions of higher education and is the author of The Negro in America 1960-80.

---

third-degree decency, mercy second-degree decency, and walking humbly with God first-degree decency. I think he meant them to be equally emphasized.

But how suggestive it is to us, when we consider it, that the first requirement ought to be to do justly. All of us recognize that justice can never make it on its own; it has to be informed and inspired and kept alert by those who rise above justice and love mercy. We know that justice and mercy do not last unless they are both inspired by our humble relationship to God.

So much truth so tightly packed into these succinct, well-chosen phrases! (It's a challenge to the Madison Avenue advertisers.) The prophet-priest who put this theology lesson together for us wasted no words: "Do justly, love mercy, and walk humbly with God." It's ethics, it's theology, it's a social thought.

You can imagine what had been going on around the prophet Micah. His people were burning animals on the altar while cheating their fellows. Seven hundred years before Christ some of them were offering their first-born children as sacrifices for their own adult sinning. They were dutiful in worship, but they robbed the poor and exploited their farm workers.

So Micah, like his fellow prophets Amos and Isaiah, spoke out against this awful distortion of religion. He pointed to irrelevance in religion: smoking altars, child sacrifices, all the efforts to placate a jealous deity. He explained that none of these things satisfied God, and he summed it all up by saying, "He hath showed thee, O man, what is good." Relevant religion is doing justly, loving mercy, and walking humbly with God.

Doing justly comes first. In its simplest expression this simply means being fair, dealing with people on the basis of equal treatment, doing to others what you would have them do to you. It's based on the assumption that no one has any right to the arbitrary assignment of preferential treatment. Everyone stands at the same level with an equal opportunity to earn the good things of life. But some persons, having impediments placed in their path, deserve some extra help in order to have equal opportunity. Justice does not mean passing out equal results willy-nilly. It doesn't mean giving everybody a bachelor of arts degree on one pretty June day or giving people who don't know medicine medical degrees. It does mean doing all we can to see that everybody has an equal opportunity to achieve equal results. This comes hard for a lot of people. It is more and more annoying to me to see how people can go to the finest universities and study some of the hard, unyielding sciences—physics and mathematics and chemistry—and then come out of that experience not knowing how to do justly and having no sensitivity for evenhandedness.

We demand all sorts of preferential treatment for ourselves, but we do not want to give it to others. We want everything our own way regardless, and we indulge in this juvenile behavior both in our private life and in our institutional life. We tolerate this in infants. Infants are interested in survival; they scream and yell when they're cold or wet or hungry or frightened. We allow a baby this high degree of egocentricity, and we even call it cute. But there's nothing cute about somebody forty-five years old who is still acting like an infant, who has never been weaned, who imposes on everyone else his or her own preferences. If you are a member of any social unit—family, club, church, neighborhood, labor union, you know there is an implicit social contract that everyone has the same right to all the benefits as everyone else, and that if anyone has any greater right, any greater share, it has been assigned for a reason that everyone can understand. You do your part, and others do theirs. This evenhanded distribution of favors and restrictions is what we call "justice," fairness.

Not long ago I finished reading a tough book by John Rawls called *A Theory of Justice*. It took him 587 pages to make it plain, but when he finished, he had said what Jesus said a long time ago, "As ye would that men should do to you, do ye also to them likewise" (Luke 6:31). This is so difficult that it has tied up the minds of philosophers for a long, long time; it does not go down easily in a competitive, cutthroat society. This *Golden Rule*, "Do unto others as you would have them do unto you," is recited sentimentally, but it has not really found a place in our culture. We would rather live by the *Silver Rule*, "Do unto others as they have already done unto you." Or the *Iron Rule*, "Do unto others as you fully expect them to do unto you." Then there's the *Bronze Rule*, "Do unto others before they do unto you." And finally, the *Copper Rule*, "Do unto others—and cut out."

Talking about justice in the city, how many of us would ever imagine that a theory of justice would apply to one who leaves a car double-parked and walks away with no note on it so that it ties up somebody for hours? How many would recognize the principle of justice applying to a situation when one blasts a stereo in a neighboring apartment all night long?

I had a young man come into one of my classes at Rutgers with a great, big, dirty, white dog with a raggedy rope tied around his neck. This was during the days of unrest on the campuses. I think that what this student had in mind was to see how relevant I could be, to see if I could tolerate a big, dirty dog in the class. (It was a class in moral values and education, by the way.) I said to him, "Do you plan to have the dog visit us for the entire period?" He said, "Why not?" And I said, "You know, the basic principle of morality is evenhandedness. Don't get fancy about existentialism; the basic principle is, I can't have anything that you cannot have, similarly situated. If you can bring your dog in here, that means everybody else can bring his or her dog in here, and how can we have class with thirty-five dogs trying to get acquainted with one another?" In all of his radical social thought, it never occurred to him that he was imposing on the rest of us by bringing his dirty dog into our classroom.

Now comes the hard part. If you really believe in justice, you cannot stop at being fair all by yourself because sometimes your little bit of fairness doesn't go very far. You can be as pure as the driven snow, but if you're living in the city and paying taxes and allowing people to be elected to office who are not going to do justly, then you haven't done justly in an institutional sense. Reinhold Niebuhr made this plain as day in his book *Moral Man and Immoral Society*. What good does it do for me to be pious and just and fair, and then go to sleep and allow institutions to be created all around me that are unfair and unjust? Our responsibility is to be just even though we may not be understood while being just.

We must learn how to lick some stamps and mail some envelopes and ring some doorbells and try to get people elected to office and try to curb some of the excesses in our society. Every now and then we look up and see people in Congress and in the White House, and nobody knows how they got there. Doing justly is not a private matter. It is not enough for Christians to be buried in their own piety and in their own sense of justice. We've got to participate and make our institutions just and fair.

Then the prophet carries us one step further. We have to recognize that behind justice comes the love of mercy. We used to have deacons pray in our churches in the South. One man had a sentence in his prayer that I thought was very meaningful. Right in the middle of his prayer he would stop and say, "Now, Father, your humble servant this morning does not pray for justice because justice does not suit my condition; I'm praying for a double portion of your mercy this morning." He did not want God to be legalistic with him; he did not want God to put the law to him; he did not want God to be only just with him; he wanted God to be more than that; he wanted God to be merciful unto him.

If you leave justice all by itself, it may not suffice because it may not be well enough informed on human needs. Think of the way we used to treat children many years ago who were born brain-damaged or mentally retarded. We thought it was just enough to keep them clean and safe. Sometimes that meant locking them up in rooms by themselves for weeks and months at a time. That's what appeared to us then to be just. And if we kept old people clean, gave them three square meals a day, we used to think that was fair and just. We did not realize that old people needed life, that they needed excitement, companionship, jokes, and music. We thought it was just and fair simply to give these people safety and succor, and that was enough. But all we've learned about psychology now tells us that the human needs for excitement and companionship go on and on all through life. Even children who appear to be mentally retarded have a margin of intelligence and awareness, and we ought to explore that margin, find out how deep it is, and see what we can do to cultivate that margin of intelligence and awareness to make their lives meaningful.

"Time makes ancient good uncouth," as Fosdick used to say. These wonderful words meant that a long time ago it might have seemed nice to have a servant you paid well and called by some respectable title but kept working sixty and eighty hours a week. We know now it is uncouth; no one has a right to deny anybody else an opportunity for fulfillment and joy and a meaningful life. So mercy cries out for expression and relevance even when justice seems to have done its best.

When I was a boy, my father used to sing in a group called The Philharmonic Glee Club in Norfolk, black men who worked in the shipyards and on the freight cars and coal cars down at Lambert's Point, table waiters and hotel bellhops who liked music. They would come together every Wednesday night in the Elks' Home and practice until way into the night. And they sang one big concert a year downtown in the city hall. It was a segregated place; my family had tickets because my daddy was in the Glee Club, but we had to sit way in the rear on benches that had no backs on them while all the white people sat up front. It looked like the worst contradiction. These men practiced all year long to give one concert in this segregated place? But they did it. All those men—barrel-chested, with melodious voices, stiff-bosomed tuxedo shirts—were immaculate, impeccable. They did their very best. They sang their hearts out to this segregated audience.

I was grown before I really got the message. I remember the last song they sang every year: "Dawn is breaking and a new day is born; the world is singing the song of the dawn. Yesterday the skies were gray, but look, this morning they are blue! The smiling sun tells everyone, 'Come, let's start life anew.' Let's all sing." And when they hit that word, they lifted the top off the place. "Hallelujah, for a new day is born. The world is singing the song of the dawn." Well, no new day had been born; there was no dawn anywhere. Things went on and on and on, but they sang with that little bit of freedom that they had. They did not get many opportunities to address this audience, and when they did get a chance, they addressed them in this prophetic way, singing about a new day that ought to be born.

Thank God that new day in that town is being born right now. When I drive through that city now and see the changes that have come about, I think about those men who went beyond what justice required. They went beyond what seemed fair. They went into the higher levels of moral effort, into mercy, one step farther. If you make me go with you one mile, then when that mile is over, I'll walk with you on my own another mile.

I don't know how we're going to solve the problems of the city unless we can find a little remnant, a kind of pilgrim cohort, of sojourners and pilgrims who go beyond what's merely fair and just and legal and go the second mile into what's merciful. Justice can't make it unless it's always being finely tuned by the sensitive spirits of those who know what ought to come next. By the grace of God, we're going to outlive the problems. And then justice will take on a new look, a new definition. Time will make ancient good uncouth.

But then, finally, the prophet said, "The end of it all is to learn to walk humbly with God." Religious experience must undergird our justice and our mercy. We are very frail people, and we are inclined to deceive ourselves. We have an enormous capacity to use our imagination to play various roles. We, among all animals, have the subjunctive mood, a sense of "might" and "may" and "perhaps." And we live with this sense of probability all the time. That's a good thing. But turn it around and see what else it does for us; it allows for enormous self-deception. And if you don't pause and worship God and the beauty of holiness, you will call things by the wrong names and think you've told the truth. This moment of silence and scrutiny before God keeps us aware that he's writing all the time, sees all you do, and hears all you say. Religious sensitivity before God will help us to know what justice is and what mercy is. These are tough days—the awful tension under which we live in the cities, the financial burden placed upon us by inflation and rising prices. And I don't think we want to try to make it without knowing how to walk humbly with God.

Down in the beautiful Blue Ridge Mountains section of Virginia, there's a marvelous phenomenon called the Natural Bridge. Flowing underneath that two-hundred-forty-four-foot arch, cut cleanly right through the Blue Ridge Mountains, there's a little stream called Cedar Creek. Now Cedar Creek doesn't look very impressive. But if you could ask the creek about itself, the creek would say, "I used to be way up high. I started cutting this arch in the mountains thousands of years ago. I just kept moving until I'd cut out the arch and then I smoothed it out as I responded to the ebb and flow of the tide of the James River from which I borrowed my strength." That's not very impressive either; in Lexington, Virginia, the James River is just another little creek.

But if you asked the James River, the river would say, "Don't look at me because I get my strength from the Chesapeake Bay around Hampton, Virginia. Oh, what turbulent tides come through there! I go down there twice every twenty-four hours and get my strength from the Chesapeake Bay." And the bay would say, "Don't look at me. I get my strength from the Atlantic Ocean, moving across a quarter of the earth's surface, lending strength to the bay, to the James River, to little Cedar Creek cutting its way through the Blue Ridge Mountains." And the ocean, if it could tell you, would say, "It is not I. I respond to gravity, to the pull of the moon, God's diminuendos and crescendos. His baton directs me, and I do what God bids me to do."

Well, you're like Cedar Creek; you can't handle that mountain all by yourself. You can't take on the world with your fists balled up, gritting your teeth, drinking booze and popping pills; you need something that brings strength from the river and the bay and the ocean and the crescendos of God's baton itself. Do justly, love mercy, and walk humbly with God. ○

His Own Clothes

Gardner C. Taylor

"And when they had mocked him, they took off the purple from him, and put his own clothes on him, and led him out to crucify him" (Mark 15:20).

Short of the cross itself and the betrayal by Judas, what the soldiers did to Jesus may well have been the most humiliating part of our Lord's suffering and death for you and me. We may be greatly wronged and deeply hurt, but we want to be able to hold on to our human dignity, the feeling that we are a part of the family of mankind. Great suffering may be visited upon us, but there can be a certain nobility, a mark of grandeur, in the way people hold their heads high and bear bravely whatever it is they must go through.

There is something uniquely cruel in being laughed at and mocked, set apart from one's fellows and made the target of ugly

Dr. Gardner C. Taylor is the pastor of the Concord Baptist Church, Brooklyn, New York, and a past president of the Progressive National Baptist Convention. He is also a former member of the Board of Education, City of New York. Dr. Taylor is a graduate of Leland College and the Oberlin Graduate School of Theology, Oberlin, Ohio. He is the recipient of honorary degrees from Benedict College, Leland College, and Albright College. He has been the Lyman Beecher lecturer and the Luccock lecturer and has taught homiletics at Colgate Rochester Divinity School, Harvard University, and Union Theological Seminary. The Republic of Liberia has conferred him Knight Commander, Order of African Redemption, and the Order of the Star of Africa.

jibes, cruel comment, and cutting laughter. One of the most painful and sinister weapons used historically against black people in this country was mockery and ridicule. Physical features were caricatured and exaggerated, and so the large, white-lipped, wide-eyed blackened faces in minstrel shows became the notion of the way black people looked and acted. I am not far enough from the experience of that mockery to be able to see the art in this kind of thing, no matter what the occasion may be. The purpose of the foot-shuffling, head-scratching, wide-grinning, ghost-frightened darky was to ridicule, scorn, and humiliate. Every southern town once had its village idiot whom children would shamefully taunt. Children who are different know how cruel such horseplay can be.

Far crueler than our own experience was the kind of scorn and ridicule that the soldiers heaped upon our Lord on the night of his crucifixion. While it may be true that the sport these members of the Praetorian guard, Pilate's military escort, made of Jesus had little venom in it, still it chills the spirit to think of the Son of God, the Savior of the world, the blessed Redeemer, being the object of the rude jokes and the broad barracks' humor of these rough and dull-witted soldiers.

The Master moved toward his death on our behalf over a road that grew constantly more steep and more terrifying. First, there was his inner agony in Gethsemane. This was followed by betrayal after which the chains were put on Jesus as a common criminal. Later that night they blindfolded our Lord and then struck him a stinging slap in the face taunting, "Prophesy. Who is it that smote thee?" Then they did spit in his face to add to the outrage. Each new assault seemed designed to outdo the last.

Following all of these things, they scourged the Lord. This painful humiliation probably took place on the platform where the trial had been held and in sight of all. The victim was stripped down to the waist and was stretched against a pillar with hands tied. The instrument of torture was a long leathern strip, studded with pieces of lead and bits of bone. The whip left lashes, and the lead and bone tore out chunks of flesh. Some died under the lash, and others emerged from the torture raving mad. Through all of these things Jesus passed in the interest of all of our souls.

All of these things, as horrible and as appalling as they are, were but preliminary and secondary to the supreme sacrifice of Calvary. So we read that after our Lord was scourged with the lash, sentence was pronounced, and it was the sentence of death by crucifixion, the most awful and painful of the Roman methods of execution. Cicero declared that it was "the most cruel and horrifying death." (William Barclay thought that the Romans picked up this method of execution from the Persians who believed the earth was sacred and wished to avoid defiling it with an evil doer.) Lifted on a cross, the condemned slowly died, and the vultures and carrion crows would dispose of the body.

The Roman ritual of condemnation and execution was fixed. Sentence was pronounced, "Illum duci ad crucem placet." The sentence was that this man should be hung on a cross. Then the judge turned to the guard and said, "I, miles, expedi crucem." Go, soldier, and prepare the cross. It was at this point that Jesus our Lord was turned over to the soldiers who formed the personal guard of Pilate as governor.

These men were hard-bitten professional soldiers who chafed at their unpleasant assignment in such a hot, fly-ridden place as Palestine and among all of those strange and offensive people. They took their pastime and sport when and where they could find them. One of their pleasures was to taunt and torture convicted criminals who cringed before them like cornered and helpless animals. The Son of God was turned over to them, and they went to work with their cruel jibes.

The whole detachment gathered in their barracks with the Savior of the world before them and, as they thought, in their hands. They stripped him of his clothes. Having picked up some thread of the charge that Jesus claimed to be a king, they jammed a reed in his hand to mock a scepter, plaited a crown made out of a thorn bush for his brow, and flung around the Lord's shoulder an old, faded red tunic, the scarlet cloak that was part of the parade uniform of the Roman soldier. All this was done to mock him as a king, and so they bowed down in ridicule as if to honor and worship him. "We will be your devotees and subjects, King Jesus. Look at us kneeling before you," and then their loud, uncouth laughter rang and echoed through the barracks.

There are still many who put cloaks of imitation honor and false respect on the Lord Jesus as surely as those soldiers put their old scarlet robe on the Savior. Such do not mean their patronizing words of respect about the Lord Jesus. You can hear them now and again. One says, "I respect and honor Jesus. His golden rule is enough religion for anyone to live by. I admire his life and believe it to be a thing of beauty. His ethics are splendid principles of conduct and human relations."

As to his church and all of that, these smart people are very lofty. "It is all right for those who need it, but I do not go to church. I do not feel the need of it, really." And so saying, they feel they have delivered themselves of something very profound and, if not profound, then chic and fashionable. Well, I had a dog, a blooded Doberman pinscher who never went to church either. I feel like answering such glib dismissal of the church for which Christ died by saying, "My dog did not go to church either. He never felt the need of it because he was a dog. Now, what is your reason?"

There are still others who put garments of mock royalty on the Lord and who call his name but who feel no deep loyalty to him, no crowning and controlling love for the Lord who has done so much for us. You may see them now and then in church, now and then among the people of Christ. They throw their leftovers at the Lord, who made us all, as a man would toss scraps to a pet dog. They are neither hot nor cold and to such the word of the Revelation applies, "I will spew thee out of my mouth" (Revelation 3:16).

There is a lot of sham religion in this country, people going through the motions for whom Christ is not a living, determining presence. Again and again people ask "What is wrong with us as a nation?" One word is the answer: godlessness. Never mind the churches and synagogues and mosques; godlessness is what is wrong with us. Never mind the public prayers and taking of oaths on the Bible. Godlessness is what is wrong with America. How does it come out? In the swagger of a gun lobby and money that stops congressmen from passing a gun law. In greed and bigotry and the attitude "anything goes." In lies and deceit in a nation that has no room for worship or things of the spirit.

You ask what is wrong with us as a people. Listen to any national telecast. See how all of our national interest in built around what some self-serving people in Washington do: crime, scams, confusion. See how little of the heart and mind, how little room for things of the spirit there is in our national telecasts. Godlessness! And until we turn to the Lord, it will not get better; it will get worse. And yes, one thing after another will go wrong.

Have I put fake garments on the Lord Jesus? Have I cloaked the Savior of the world in scarlet robes of pretense, claiming that I honor him as Lord while my heart is far from him? Do I take my faith in the Lord Jesus seriously? Am I willing, as George Eliot put it, to sacrifice anything for him as long as the result is not unpleasant?

And then we read that when the soldiers had tired of their ugly game of ridicule and making sport of the Son of God, they took off the old scarlet tunic and put his own clothes back on him. This was the final preparation for crucifixion. They put on our Lord his own clothes. And "his own clothes" say worlds to us. We need to see him as he is, "in his own clothes," not mocked and ridiculed by false respect and pious hypocrisy. When we see the Lord "in his own clothes," in his true character and force, we see someone who makes us cry out for forgiveness and for his good favor and approval. Looking at Jesus as he is, we see ourselves as we are.

When our Christ is not mocked by false garments of respectable sneer or false enthusiasm, when we see him in his own clothes as he is, we want to do better. Dr. Donald Shelby, the California United Methodist preacher, has told of a terrible storm on Lake Michigan in which a ship was wrecked near the shore. A Northwestern University student, Edmond Spenser, went into the raging water again and again and single-handedly rescued seventeen people. When friends carried him to his room, nearly exhausted and faint, he kept asking them, "Did I do my best?" In the presence of Christ we ask, "Lord, did I do my best?" I am a preacher and each time I preach I must ask, "Lord, did I do my best?" Officer, choir member, usher, did you do your best?

Jesus in his own clothes going to Calvary did his best. His garments on that lonely hill were rolled in blood, making understandable the old cry of Isaiah, "Who is this that cometh from Edom, with dyed garments from Bozrah? this that is glorious in his apparel, travelling in the greatness of his strength? (Isaiah 63:1). We ask, "Wherefore art thou red in thine apparel, and thy garments [thy clothes] like him that treadeth in the winefat?" (Isaiah 63:2). And he answers, "I have trodden the winepress alone. . . . For the day of vengeance is in mine heart, and the year of my redeemed is come" (Isaiah 63:3-4).

In his own clothes he went to Calvary and made everything all right, not temporarily all right but for always. At Calvary Christ was at his best. Nothing had been left undone. On no other day does Jesus have to go back to finish his work at Calvary. This he did once. ". . . Now once in the end of the world hath he appeared to put away sin by the sacrifice of himself. . . . So Christ was once offered to bear the sins of many . . ." (See Hebrews 9:26-28). He died in his own clothes as Savior and Redeemer. Once for all. It is all right now. The crooked way has been made straight; we may arise and shine for our light is come. It is all right now.

We shall see him yet in other clothes. Ellen White, the prophetess of Seventh Day Adventism, pictures that day when Christ shall appear with an old, faded red cloak around his shoulders, no longer mocked by soldiers, no longer wearing simple garments of this earth. Every eye shall see him. We will see him as Heaven's king, victor over death, hell, and the grave, the admired of angels. Every eye shall see him. Ten thousand times ten thousand and thousands and thousands of angels and the triumphant sons and daughters of God will escort him. His raiment will outshine the sun. And on his vesture, his garment, a name will be written, "King of Kings and Lord of Lords." Shall we not shout his name who has lifted us to heights sublime and made us his own people forever? ○

'What Doth Hinder Me?'

James S. Tinney

Acts 8:26-40

Introduction

In the eighth chapter of the book of Acts, Saint Luke tells one of the most important stories in all the New Testament. It is the story of a black eunuch's conversion. Here, in the middle of stories about the conversion of three thousand persons, miracles of healing, the arrest of apostles Peter and John, and the death of two prominent church leaders named Ananias and Sapphira, we discover a follow-up story to the day of Pentecost. (In journalism we would call it a "side-bar" story, somewhat removed from the major epochal event in the news

Dr. James S. Tinney is the assistant professor of journalism, School of Communication, Howard University. He is president of the Black Religious Writers' Association, board member of the Society of Blacks in Religious Communication, a member of the Afro-American History Group of the American Academy of Religion and of the Society of Pentecostal Studies. He is a graduate of Howard University, Washington, D.C., where he received his B.S. in journalism, M.A. in education, and Ph.D. in political science. He is the founder of the Pentecostal Coalition for Human Rights. *Eternity* magazine listed Dr. Tinney as one of the fifty most influential evangelical thinkers in America.

but related to it as a footnote of human interest.)

Not only is this story easily overlooked—sandwiched as it is between these other major events and the conversion event of the apostle Paul that immediately follows it—but it is sometimes dismissed for other reasons as well. Its major character is not given a name; its Christian subject is not an apostle, but a lay-evangelist; its noteworthy baptismal confession statement ("I believe that Jesus Christ is the Son of God.") is a later addition not found in the earliest manuscripts; and it is a story without a conclusion, ending abruptly with no further details about what happened immediately afterward to either Philip or the one converted. In spite of these detractions, the story is of special relevance to all persons who are members of a racial or sexual minority, to all the socially and religiously and politically oppressed persons of the world. So we retell it with the hope that its message will stir us once more.

It is hoped that there will occur a new dimension to this retelling, however, since Luke's account tells the story from Philip's point of view while it will now be told from the point of view of the oppressed, the people of salvation.

I. The People of Salvation

Important details, even major facts of intrinsic value, are omitted from Luke's drama precisely because he was not able to assign them proper merit or interpret them properly. He was, after all, white, and so he emphasized the role of Philip who was of the same race. And he was an "insider," a respected member of the clergy class, plus a Gentile Christian; hence, he was interested in the story only with respect to the experience of his fellow clergyman, Philip, rather than with great regard for how a Jew (or Jewish convert) felt and experienced what happened. This is not to say that the apostle Luke was intentionally one-sided or purposefully neglectful (or even racist). But male-dominated, male-written, male-interpreted history suffers from a certain inherent deficit of understanding that has affected even the way biblical history has come down to us. Wouldn't it have been much more edifying if we also had records of women writing about how they felt when they heard the angelic annunciation and sat at Jesus' feet in Bethany and looked up at their child being crucified and discovered the resurrection?

Even as we must reconstruct the gospel from the standpoint of women, so we must reconstruct it from the vantage of peoples of color, for these are the true subjects of salvation and deliverance: the oppressed of the world. Which is not to say that "straight" white men cannot also be saved, but, like the rich young ruler in Jesus' day, their salvation comes only by deliverance from these very aspects of identity and privilege that they hold dear, and "few there be that find it." The conversion of the Ethiopian eunuch, however, is about one of the oppressed minorities who "heard Jesus gladly."

An Ethiopian. The Scriptures are very clear about the racial identity of the protagonist in our story. He was an Ethiopian, or (as the Greek reads) "a man from Ethiopia." He was black, not simply a diasporan Hebrew residing in Africa; for the word Ethiopia was used in Bible times as a name for all of Africa itself, and consequently, all black persons were called Ethiopians.

While Luke was not careful enough to give the story's major character a name, nonbiblical literary sources have done so. In the modern nation-state known as Ethiopia, tradition says his name was Juda, a proper name for a black Jew.[1]

Juda knew what racial discrimination was. On his own continent he had suffered at the hands of invading white Persians, white Greeks and Romans, and even lighter-complexioned persons of Mediterranean or mixed descent, who repeatedly invaded Africa's shores, setting up colonial governments and pushing black rulers further south. He also had experienced prejudice at the hands of other Jews, those who resided in Jerusalem itself and whose parental lineage was composed of followers of the Jewish religion as far back as they could remember. Every time he went to Jerusalem, he felt freshly the sharp barbs of names like "proselyte," "foreigner," and worse. While others went into the holy sanctuary of the temple, he was segregated and forbidden to go further than the outer court reserved for Gentiles. Furthermore, even his nephews and nieces, the next generation of African Jews, would not be any better off than he. For ten generations to come, his family's posterity would be castigated and oppressed as "proselytes of the gate"[2] (meaning, they could go little further than inside the gate of the temple yard). It is not difficult to understand, given this discrimination, why Juda would be open to considering a change of religion once he came into contact with any Christian.

This is not to say, however, that Juda was not a sincere believer in the Jewish faith. As a child, he had heard his mother tell him the story of the great Makeda, Queen of the South (or of Sheba).[3] God rewarded Queen Makeda and the Ethiopians by giving to Africa the Ark of the Covenant through the machinations of some of Solomon's young rebels.[4] Further, God had promised that one day all of Africa "shall soon stretch out her hands unto God" (Psalm 68:31). And when Juda's mother kissed him goodnight, she often quoted the promise of God that read, "Blessed be [Ethiopia], my people" (Isaiah 19:25).

A Chamberlain for the Queen. As the New Testament story unfolds, Juda is serving as a chamberlain for a queen. The word chamberlain has two meanings, and Juda fulfilled them both. On the one hand, it meant a person who was in charge of a treasury of money; on the other, it referred to a person who was in charge of a queen's bedroom.

Because Juda was an effeminate man with neither the social approval nor the hard-driving ambition necessary to pose a genuine threat to the throne, the Queen felt justified in bestowing upon him "high office and great responsibility," which extended beyond that of keeping charge over her boudoir. Therefore, she entrusted Juda with power over her personal treasury and gave him the authority of a prince.[5] This status Juda did not enjoy because he had royal lineage or even because of natural attainments but because he was a slave.[6] Rather than a badge of freedom, therefore, his was a badge of oppression. Because of his intelligence and skills, he became a servant in the "big house"; because of his sexual status, he was still a slave.

A Eunuch. Juda was privileged in many ways, without a doubt. Other eunuchs in both Africa and Jerusalem were not so fortunate as to become a chamberlain. As keeper of the Queen's own bedchamber, he was her closest company. Perhaps he was even the supervisor of a retinue of eunuchs who assisted him in the care and keeping of the palace's bedrooms.

While Juda's faith in Judaism was complete, the suffering he endured socially as a homosexual was compounded by the religious discrimination afflicted upon him. Not only was he a "proselyte of the gate" because he was African; he was also a second-class proselyte because he was a eunuch. He suffered double indemnity, and the same religion that oppressed him as a black man also oppressed him as a homosexual. Many times Juda had longed for the opportunity to belong fully to God's house, but the Mosaic law barred eunuchs not only from the priesthood (Leviticus 21:20) but also from membership in the congregation itself (Deuteronomy 23:1). No wonder Juda was willing to entertain the new Christian religion.

II. The Process of Salvation

But what brought Juda more than two hundred miles from his home to Jerusalem? No doubt the major purpose was to transact business for the Queen in much the same manner as servants of Makeda, Queen of Sheba, sent servants or slaves to Jerusalem earlier. But there are those who think that Juda's trip may have been some kind of religious pilgrimage.

A Fascinating Sect. Unfit for full participation as a Jew, it is unlikely that Juda came such a long way simply to participate in the Jewish festival of Shavuot (also known as Pentecost in the Greek language). Nevertheless, if the time span of the Lukan record can be accepted, it is probable that only a few days had lapsed between the day of Pentecost and the Acts 8 incident. Thus Juda was likely present in Jerusalem at the time of Pentecost, and may even have seen the Pentecostal descent of the Spirit in the Upper Room. Even if he only heard about that event, he would have viewed it as similar to the long-standing practice of spirit possession and speaking in tongues that characterized African traditional religion.

His attention was also drawn to the new sect called Christians because of other rumors he had heard about them. For instance, he was amazed at the way in which the first waves of the Christian movement had embraced persons of all races. There had been blacks present in Jerusalem for the descent of the Spirit in the Upper Room; women were preaching and prophesying; and economic classism was being undermined by the common sharing of goods and property.

What is more, the man the Christians spoke of as their Messiah had said good things about eunuchs. Jesus had talked about certain eunuchs who were ". . . so born from their mother's womb. . ." (Matthew 19:12). And he had encouraged acceptance of eunuchs by stating, "He that is able . . . let him receive it" (Matthew 19:12). In other words, "Let the man embrace it as a gift" rather then negate it as a cross.

A Handsome Stranger. Juda didn't realize it at that point, but the Spirit of God was at work in his life, leading him toward a liberated life. It was that same Spirit who led him, almost without thinking, to purchase an expensive scroll of the Alexandrian Greek version of the Hebrew Scriptures. How thankful he was that he had the money to buy it and the knowledge of that language to read it. The Holy Spirit was also suggesting to him the way he should travel back to Africa, now that important matters in Jerusalem were concluded. "Take the desert road to Gaza," a strange intuition told him.

The road home had other advantages to it as well. For one thing, it was less frequently traveled; by taking it, Juda would escape the other travelers who would seek to satisfy their curiosity by staring at him, calling him a "freak," and otherwise interrupting his privacy. So Juda called his large retinue of servants together for last minute instructions and then climbed inside a covered chariot used for courtly travel, unlike the open, war chariot others sometimes used.

While the entourage traveled away from Jerusalem, Juda read aloud (as his religion required) from his new scroll. Suddenly— seemingly out of nowhere—another traveler appeared. It was customary for sojourners to attach themselves to caravans or larger parties winding their way through the desert, and so the white man was welcomed as he joined the procession. Calling him into his carriage, Juda soon discovered that the man was a Christian and his name was Philip. When Philip asked if the meaning of the scroll was clear, Juda invited Philip to give his own explanation, not because Juda didn't know what he was reading but because he was inquisitive about other possible interpretations and, perhaps more important, because he wanted to find out more about Philip himself.

What could have been a culturally imperialistic attempt on the part of a stranger was changed into a genuine interpersonal contact by the specific elements of the mission. All heterosexuals who attempt to minister to lesbians and gays and all whites who attempt to minister to blacks and other peoples of color should note the special circumstances that made this encounter a genuinely human and mutual one. First, Philip had been in constant contact with peoples of color, having met Juda shortly after a revival among the Samaritans. (He was not on a temporary excursion into the ghetto.) Second, Philip's contacts were broad enough to reach many classes; the Samaritans were viewed as "lower class," and Juda was definitely "upper class" by comparison. (Philip was not concerned about reaching middle-class people like himself, nor was he on a search for exotic converts.) Third, he began his mission only upon invitation of Juda. (He did not presume to "bogard" into another's personal life, as if he had some special authority or divine calling to do so.) Fourth, he was content to leave Juda, as a new convert, to develop his Christian faith and life in his own African context. (He did not try to make Juda perpetually dependent upon him.) All who would attempt to reach racial and sexual minorities with the gospel should take cues from this early Christian inter-cultural witness.

A Eunuchal God. Most important, from a theological viewpoint, Juda's interest in this new religion he had heard about and his experience of religious oppression as a black Jewish proselyte and a black homosexual became an opportunity for conversion because the gospel, the Good News, was that God identifies with the oppressed.

Not only does God identify with the oppressed, but, Philip noted also, God in Jesus Christ became oppressed. Here, said Philip, explaining Isaiah's prophecy, was God physically mutilated. If God had suffered in physical torture, then surely God would love and understand and provide deliverance from oppression for eunuchs as well.

Even further, the gospel emphasized that Jesus was led unwillingly, was silent because there was no one to hear or help, was humiliated, was denied justice, had no children, and had life itself taken away. Jesus' experience was so familiar; homosexuals are humiliated by name-calling and threats and assaults and rape, are denied justice in every institution from the courts to the churches, often have no children to love or keep, and are, in a desperate but unpublished conspiracy of murders, separated from life on earth itself. And it was familiar to peoples of color who are led in slavery into a strange land, are silenced by whips and burning crosses and tar-feathers and lynching, are humiliated and robbed of personhood in the view of friends and families, are denied justice on every hand, and are robbed of children who are sold "down the river" into drugs, wars, and prisons.

The life of a eunuch might be on the edge of fate's extremity, but God has entered the world of all kinds of eunuchs, and God has in Jesus Christ become a eunuch as well. Even more, God has declared war on the enemies of eunuchs and promised a victory celebration with mercy for the oppressed and judgment for the oppressors. In response, what could Juda possibly do but stop the chariot, in faith be baptized, and embrace this beautiful stranger who bore witness to the God of eunuchs.

III. The Promise of Salvation

The beautiful thing about this story is that sexuality, far from being a deterrent to finding or following God, is instead a way in which God demonstrates the incarnation.

There was no demand that Juda get rid of sexual desire as a prerequisite to obtaining God's favor. Neither was it necessary for Juda to forget the sexual past or somehow pledge a different sexual future in order for God to bring salvation and the gift of the Spirit. Indeed, nothing was mentioned about internal states related either to intensity or direction of desire or about external states related either to race or physical condition in the Gospel presentation. Rather, it was God's identification with and affirmation of Juda that brought conversion. There was no special requirement peculiar to Juda's physical or emotional being, nor was there mandated any change in his natural state. There was, instead, a better promise (also found in the same scroll of Isaiah that Juda was reading that day in his carriage): "For thus said the LORD unto the eunuchs . . . unto them will I give in mine house and within my walls a place and a name better than of sons and of daughters: I will give them an everlasting name, that shall not be cut off" (Isaiah 56:4-5).

And history records that it was so. On Juda's return home, the Queen was also converted, and, in turn, she dedicated to Jesus Christ an ancient temple built by the Queen of Sheba.[7] Ethiopian tradition claims that Juda became an apostle to Africa, Arabia and Ceylon.[8]

With such a promise and so great a salvation our only possible response (like that of Juda) would be, "What doth hinder me from being baptized?" ○

End Notes

[1] William L. Hansberry, *Pillars in Ethiopian History: The William Leo Hansberry African History Notebook*, ed. Joseph E. Harris (Washington: Howard University Press, 1974), pp. 63-64.

[2] Everett F. Harrison, ed., *Baker's Dictionary of Theology* (Grand Rapids: Baker Book House, 1960), p. 426.

[3] Hansberry, *op. cit.*, pp. 45-49.

[4] *Ibid.*, p. 48.

[5] Charles W. Carter, ed., *Wesleyan Bible Commentary* (Kansas City: Beacon Hill Press, 1960), vol. 4, p. 358.

[6] Ralph Earle, ed., *Adam Clarke's Commentary on the Entire Bible* (Grand Rapids: Baker Book House, 1974), vol. 1, p. 190.

[7] Hansberry, *op. cit.*, p. 64.

[8] Frank M. Snowden Jr., *Blacks in Antiquity* (Cambridge, Mass.: Harvard University Press, 1970), p. 206.

Additional Sermon Resources

Published by Judson Press

Best Black Sermons, *Edited by William Philpot.* Sermons that emphasize black dignity and proclaim God's power.

Biblical Dimensions of Church Growth, *Jitsuo Morikawa.* Nine sermons and Bible studies on the meanings of growth.

Biblical Faith and the Black American, *Latta R. Thomas.* Calls upon black Americans to rediscover the liberating power of the biblical message.

Broken Bread in a Broken World, *Brian A. Greet.* Takes readers back to the Upper Room during the first Communion.

Children's Moment, The, *Julius Fischbach.* Fifty-two story sermons for children arranged for a 12-month calendar.

Children's Time in Worship, *Arline J. Ban.* Practical ideas for involving children in corporate worship. Extensive resources section for pastors.

Christ Is Victor, *Edited by W. Glynn Evans.* Twenty-three sermons by prominent preachers, based on the Easter theme.

Contemporary Biblical Interpretation for Preaching, *Ronald J. Allen.*

Creating Fresh Images for Preaching, *Thomas H. Troeger.* Describes a process for using personal imagination and creativity in developing provocative imagery in sermons.

Dialogic Style in Preaching, *George W. Swank.* Views the sermon as but one phase of an extended conversation which begins before the worship service and continues after the preaching has ended.

Dramatic Narrative in Preaching, *David M. Brown.* Easy steps any preacher can use to prepare and present an effective dynamic, first-person telling of a biblical story.

Here They Stand: Biblical Sermons from Eastern Europe, *Compiled and edited by Lewis A. Drummond.* Twenty-three sermons preached from pulpits behind the iron curtain.

Hymn and Scripture Selection Guide, *Compiled by Donald A. Spencer.* Cross-reference of Scripture and hymns, with 12,000 references for 380 hymns.

Images of the Black Preacher, *H. Beecher Hicks, Jr.* Explores the forces that have influenced the multifaceted images of the black preacher as a basis for determining the future direction of the profession.

In Step with Jesus, *Norman Paullin.* Eleven sermons. Drawn from the Bible and a wide range of human experience.

Interpreting God's Word in Black Preaching, *Warren H. Stewart, Sr.*

Making of the Sermon, The, *T. Harwood Pattison.* The art of preaching and the techniques of sermon building.

Manual on Preaching, *Milton Crum, Jr.* Offers a detailed process for constructing sermons which speak to the needs of the people.

My Lord Speaks, *Stephen Benko.* Interprets the seven last words of Jesus on the cross. Explores their linguistic, textual, and historical significance.

Myths That Mire the Ministry, *Harold A. Carter.* How false images of the minister as a spiritual leader and a person distract pastor and members from following Jesus.

Outstanding Black Sermons, *J. Alfred Smith, Sr., editor.* Covering a variety of themes, these selected sermons are helpful for all pastors.

Outstanding Black Sermons, Volume 2, *Walter B. Hoard, editor.*

Postscript to Preaching, *Gene E. Bartlett.* A pastor looks ahead with enthusiasm to the urgent task of preaching the good news to a secular society.

Preaching According to Plan, *Glenn H. Asquith.* Stresses the planning for sermons over extended periods of time.

Preaching to Suburban Captives, *Alvin C. Porteous.* Liberating theology for middle-class families of suburbia.

Proclaiming the Acceptable Year: Sermons from the Perspective of Liberation Theology, *Justo L. Gonzalez, editor.* Sermons from leaders in third world churches which demonstrate commitment to the gospel as the Good News of freedom from sin and oppression.

Sayings and Doings of Jesus, *LaRue A. Loughhead.* Dramatic presentations of Jesus' miracles and parables retold in the first person. Innovative sermon resource involving the congregation.

Sermon on the Mount, *Clarence Jordan.* An interpretation of Christ's sermon that explores today's problems.

"Somebody's Calling My Name," *Wyatt Tee Walker.* Detailed history of black sacred music and its relationship to social change.

Struggle for Meaning, The, *William Powell Tuck, editor.* Seventeen sermons of hope deeply rooted in the reality of Christian faith.